THE F
LEADERSHIP

NO ONE
TALKS
ABOUT

BOB WOOLVERTON

Bob Woolverton

TOP TIER
LEADERSHIP TRAINING

Project Management/Editorial Services: Amy Rose Consulting, Inc.
Composition: Richa Bargotra/Kia Technologies
Cover Design: Diana Coe/Crone Communications

Cover and Part Opener images: Andrey Kusmin/stock.adobe.com
Interior images used under license from Shutterstock.com:
Figure 4.1 Plateresca/Shutterstock.com
Figure 4.2 Plateresca/Shutterstock.com
Figure 4.3 Plateresca/Shutterstock.com
Figure 4.4 Plateresca/Shutterstock.com
Figure 10.4 Picsfive/Shutterstock.com
Unnumbered figure, Page 78 Tish1/Shutterstock.com
Unnumbered figure, Page 96 ArtMari/Shutterstock.com
Unnumbered figure, Page 97 Yuri Samsonov/Shutterstock.com
Unnumbered figure, Page 106 VikaSuh/Shutterstock.com
Figure 25.1 Plateresca/Shutterstock.com

DISCLAIMER AND TERMS OF USE
The author and publisher make no representation or assurances with
respect to the exactness, applicability, appropriateness, or wholeness of
the accompanying materials and the contents of this book. The information contained herein is strictly for informative and development
purposes.

ISBN: 978-1-7344360-0-6 (Paperback)
ISBN: 978-1-7344360-1-3 (eBook)

MW00618282

CONTENTS

ABOUT THE AUTHOR

Bob Woolverton worked in law enforcement for 34 years, with the majority of that time spent in high-level leadership positions. One day he had an epiphany moment—he realized he knew nothing about leadership, even though he was in a leadership position. He was a great manager—but a lousy leader. Since then, Bob has become obsessed with learning about leadership. He has read every book he could get his hands on and attended every class with "leadership" in the title.

At age 56, while working full-time as a Police Captain, Bob went back to college and obtained a Bachelor of Science degree in Management and Leadership. After that achievement, he immediately continued his academic pursuits, and at age 58 obtained his Master of Science degree, also in Management and Leadership. During this same time, he became a certified leadership instructor at the Washington State Criminal Justice Center, where he teaches a 40-hour course titled Middle Management. Bob summarizes the curriculum of the middle management class as being a 40-hour crash course in organizational change, focusing on Executive-Level leadership. Additionally, Bob is a graduate of the FBI National Academy, Session #183.

Bob says the following about leadership and organizational change:

> Leadership is nothing if not about change. If there is no change, one could argue there is no leadership—leadership is not about maintaining the status quo. A person who keeps their hand on the rudder of the ship and never changes direction is not a leader—they're just along for the ride. The same can be accomplished by tying a rope to the rudder. A leader is someone who envisions a better tomorrow and sees a way to guide the organization to that vision.
>
> When discussing leadership, many people focus solely on the relationship between the leader and follower. They miss the concept that leadership includes leading toward something—leading toward a compelling vision of something the organization aspires to become or aspires to achieve.

In his new career, Bob continues to be a leadership instructor at the state police academy and also leads his own company, Top Tier Leadership Training. At Top Tier Leadership Training, Bob provides training seminars that teach mid-level managers and executives how to become better leaders. Bob is also a motivational leadership speaker providing keynote speeches at association meetings and speaking to youth groups. Bob aspires to be a positive change-agent when it comes to leadership training. His personal motto is Lead, Teach, and Inspire.

Learn more at www.TopTierLeadershipTraining.com

DEDICATION

To Lisa, who supported me during my academic years and so much more. We were both working full-time, and I spent every spare minute outside of work buried in my studies. You encouraged me and made it possible for me to be buried in my studies for all those years. You took care of all the household stuff and put the Honey-Do list on the back burner for nearly three years. Without your support, encouragement, and wisdom, my graduations may never have come to fruition.

To my dear friend Eve, your encouragement awakened the belief in me that I possessed something unique to offer the leadership world, and that I had the entrepreneurial spirit within me to make this a reality. Seriously, I would have never created Top Tier Leadership Training without your confidence in me, along with your steadfast support and encouragement.

And to my dear friend Janet who helped me carry this book across the finish line. Your consistently positive support, your hours and hours of reviewing, editing, and proposing new perspectives were invaluable. It was your recommendation that led me to finding my amazing project manager. Without your encouragement and guidance, this book may still be one of those "someday" pipe dreams.

The words "Thank You" don't even begin to convey my gratitude to all three of you. I wouldn't have and couldn't have done it without you.

INTRODUCTION

Even Charismatic Leaders Can Be Lousy Leaders—Lousy Leadership is Everywhere

When you attend a typical leadership class, one of the exercises in the course may be to list the traits or characteristics of a good leader. I've seen this done dozens of times, and the list usually includes honesty and integrity, charisma, vulnerability, confidence, commitment, passion, excellent communication, decision-making capabilities, empathy, resilience, humility, emotional intelligence, the ability to inspire others, etc. The list can continue indefinitely. However, with a list like this people get confused and mistakenly believe if they can master all of these traits, or exhibit most of these traits, they will be a good leader. Wrong! These traits all relate to the interpersonal part of leadership, the "relationship" between the leader and the follower. While the relationship is an integral part of leadership, it is not *leadership* itself. It's the *interpersonal* part of leadership, and while valuable, it's not a necessary component of good leadership.

I have worked for leaders who were great people. Everyone in the organization loved them as the person they were. And yet they were horrible leaders. Why? Because they weren't "leading."

Some of the greatest leaders in the tech industry were known for being difficult to work with, they ranked low on interpersonal skills, and yet they were considered great leaders of their day.

Why? Because they had a compelling vision of the future. They had a vision that others could conceptualize, and it inspired so much belief in the leader's vision that followers committed themselves to help make the vision of the future become a reality. This is what's called the *conceptual* part of leadership—having a compelling vision of the future, a vision of what the organization aspires to accomplish or aspires to become. Because the vision is so persuasive other people who have a similar belief come on board to fulfill their personal need to be part of something bigger than themselves and make the leader's vision a reality. They don't commit to the vision for you as the leader; they do it for themselves because their view of the world is like yours. They believe in what you believe.

Nearly everyone has some calling in life. There is something within them that intrinsically drives them. I have seen nurses in the healthcare industry who were amazing at their jobs. To me, these nurses were like angels sent from above. They displayed an incredible amount of compassion in their work. I could never do that type of work with the level of compassion and kindness they share with their patients. My DNA is not wired the same way their DNA is wired. My DNA is wired toward public service, and service to others, but in a different way than the nurses I have seen. Some people aspire to become architects. Some people aspire to be firefighters or police officers; others aspire to creative lines of work. You usually don't see someone who wants to be an architect apply to be a firefighter—it's not their calling. The role of a firefighter does not appeal to them intrinsically the way architecture calls to them, which brings me to the whole point of this book. As a leader, you must become very, very clear on why your organization exists, *and* what you aspire to achieve (or aspire to become) as an organization. This is the conceptual part of leadership that no one talks about. When you become very clear on why your organization exists and what your organization aspires to achieve, people who have similar beliefs will be knocking on your door to contribute to your larger purpose.

Before September 11, 2001, young people walking into military recruiting offices were mostly interested in earning money for college or finding a full-time job. After 9/11, people of all ages were contacting military recruiting offices, not for college tuition or a full-time job, but rather for patriotic reasons. And it wasn't just young people. People in their fifties were coming back to re-enlist. All of these people, young and old, were intrinsically motivated to serve their country—to be part of something greater than themselves.[1]

Leadership within your organization is the same: It's about identifying that larger purpose related to your organization and providing direction toward that ultimate goal. People who share your passion for why your organization exists will sign up because they intrinsically believe in your vision. This is the necessary foundation of leadership that no one talks about. You can have all the traits and characteristics of a great leader, but if you're not *leading toward* something meaningful—then you're a nice person everyone likes— but you're not a leader. Imagine if you could be a nice person everyone loves and admires, *and* you were a great leader. This book will help you get there.

Almost daily, I meet people who quit their jobs. They didn't leave their company; they left a lousy leader. Recently I was in an Italian restaurant in Bellevue, Washington. Directly behind me was a table of eight women who were celebrating something. My first clue that it was a celebration was when one of the women, with the waitress standing by her side, called out, "Who wants a shot of tequila?" It was Friday evening, and I was in a celebratory mood, so I sheepishly turned around and raised my hand as though I was saying, "Please, Ma'am, may I have a shot of tequila too?" My gesture got a friendly laugh from the women at the table, but no shot of tequila.

---

1   Daniel, Lisa. "Recruiters Recall Patriotism of Post-9/11 America." U.S. Department of Defense, https://archive.defense.gov/news/newsarticleaspx?id=65272. Accessed 19 Jan. 2020.

Later, as the women were preparing to leave, the woman who made the original tequila announcement came over to me and put her hand on my shoulder as she apologized for not buying me a shot. We laughed, and I asked what they were celebrating. The woman replied, "Six of us quit our jobs today."

I asked why they quit their jobs, and the response was nearly simultaneous and was unanimous, "Because our boss sucks!"

I told the woman it was unfortunate we hadn't met earlier because she could have given my business card to her boss. She asked, "What do you do?" as she reached for the business card I was offering to her.

I told her, "I teach sucky bosses to be less sucky." The entire table erupted into laughter as the woman immediately handed my business card to the only two women at the table who hadn't quit their jobs yet, almost like she was offering them a lifeline saying, "Here, you need this."

Although we all had a good laugh—from a business perspective, think of the fiscal and operational impact to the business that just lost six employees that day—all due to poor leadership. What would happen in your organization if six employees quit on the same day? I can only imagine what this boss, who just had six employees leave, is probably saying to themself, "Good riddance, they were all problem employees anyway." Were *they* the problem employees? At the FBI Academy, the instructional staff would call this "a clue." It might be time for this boss to check their ego at the door and take a serious look in the mirror.

Earlier that same day, I met a man who had just quit his job after working at his company for only three months. He told me the same story. He had left due to poor leadership. I could relate because I had done the exact same thing a year earlier: I had quit my job due to poor leadership. I loved my job, and I would have probably stayed for another five or seven years, however, I had the financial ability to leave, and I couldn't tolerate the poor leadership any longer, which is why I left. We called it retirement, but really, I just changed careers. I didn't retire. Within two weeks, I was so busy I didn't know how I had ever had time in my day to go to that last job. The reality was that the leadership at the previous job was so poor, I had left a job I loved, a job I would have continued to do for many more years to come. In my case, my employer had just paid tuition reimbursement for me to get my bachelor's degree and my master's degree. So, with me quitting (quitting the lousy leadership), they had lost their return on their investment of that tuition money, and they had lost 34 years of institutional knowledge and experience. What was the cost of poor leadership in that case? It was very, very expensive.

Now don't get me wrong, I live in a glass house, so I'm not casting stones. Poor leadership is everywhere. In my career, I was a poor leader too. I didn't know anything about leadership, and leadership wasn't being mentored in my organization because no one above me knew anything about leadership either. But here's the most significant difference between them and me. When I realized I was a poor leader, I put my ego aside (that's the biggest challenge for most leaders—checking your ego at the door) and worked hard to learn how to be a good leader. I went back to college and got a bachelor's degree and a master's degree in Management and Leadership and became a leadership instructor at the state police academy. To this day, I still work hard to be a better leadership instructor. I read new books and research articles, and I'm continually updating my curriculum to make every class I teach better than the previous class. A good leader is a life-long learner. You will never know everything, and everyone you meet in life knows something you don't know. The day you think you know everything is the day you're done being a leader.

In this book, I will walk you through theories of motivation so that you can understand why your followers choose the behaviors they choose—and most importantly—why they choose to follow you as their leader. I'll also walk you through the concept of looking at your organization as a collection of systems and processes and recognize that more often than not, when there's a problem in our organization it's usually not a people problem, it's a systems problem. And usually, the problem is caused by a system *we* created. Because we created it, we can fix it. And finally, I'll show you how to blend these concepts into the conceptual part of leadership that cultivates the intrinsic motivation of your followers. To be an effective leader, you must understand this conceptual part of leadership, which is why I wrote this book. I am not going to teach you how to be charismatic or vulnerable with your followers because there are thousands of books out there that focus on that essential purpose, however, there are very few books that talk about what we're going to cover here. The conceptual part of leadership is the part of leadership no one talks about...so let's get started!

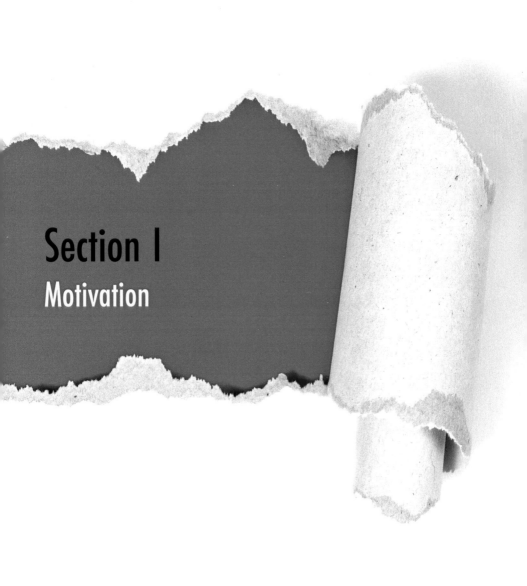

Section I
Motivation

CHAPTER 1

Why Consider Theories of Motivation?

One day I was collaborating with Mike, a colleague of mine, to create new written expectations for the first-level supervisors in the division we managed. We were both police captains in a medium-sized municipal police department in the suburbs of Seattle, Washington. Mike was responsible for the night shift, and I was responsible for the day shift. We regularly collaborated on the direction and expectations for our division, and we were generally in sync with each other 99% of the time. And when we weren't in sync, we had an excellent history of patiently and professionally working through our differences of opinion. Although admittedly on infrequent occasions, the patient and professional parts were sometimes slow to emerge in our debates.

As we drafted our expectations for our supervisors, one of those differences of opinion surfaced. The difference of opinion occurred in the very first section of our draft. The following image, Figure 1.1, is a copy of the first section of our new document.

PATROL OPERATIONS DIVISION

EXPECTATIONS FOR SERGEANTS

In addition to the expectations set forth for all members of the Patrol Operations Division, sergeants are expected to adhere to the following in principle and practice:

Lead, Teach & Inspire

- Set objectives and goals that are meaningful and contribute to a larger purpose.
- Provide inspirational motivation – provide officers with a sense of meaning and challenge to their work, convey the positive influence and benefit of their work.
- Provide intellectual stimulation – encourage officers to respectfully question assumptions, explore new ideas and methods, and develop their own decision-making skills.
- Provide idealized influence – model behaviors your people will strive to emulate or mirror.
- Provide individualized consideration – give special attention to each officer's need for achievement and growth.

Figure 1.1

We agreed, all of these bullet points sound like powerful intentions emphasizing the value employees bring to the workplace and cultivating their growth. However, Mike took exception to the first three words of the second bullet point—*Provide inspirational motivation.*

Mike firmly believed that employees must arrive at work already motivated to do a good job. He asserted that the workplace can't "motivate" an employee; the employee must come to work already self-motivated to put in a good day's work.

My argument was just the opposite. I asserted that the workplace can indeed provide an environment for motivation; an environment that connects with an employee's sense of purpose and accomplishment that creates intrinsic motivation, which results in employees who are committed to the cause of the organization and will give their full effort to support that cause. Our debate regarding these two differing viewpoints continued for some time.

In my classes, I present this scenario to the students and ask them, "does the workplace create an environment for motivation, or does the employee need to come to work already self-motivated?" The discussions that follow are interesting to listen to. Usually, after a 20-minute debate at their respective tables, the class is evenly divided into thirds. One-third believes the employee needs to come to work already self-motivated. One-third believes the workplace creates an environment for motivation and one-third say it's a combination of both. What do you think? What's your answer to this question?

As we progress through this book, your answer to this question may or may not change—however, one thing is for sure: the way you evaluate your answer to this question <u>will</u> change! You will have substantive criteria upon which to base your answer, and you'll be able to leverage that criteria as supporting arguments as you explain your decision to others.

Before we go much further, we should define the term "motivation." When you look on the Web, there are dozens of definitions, i.e., *the reason or reasons one has for acting or behaving in a particular way.* Or *the general desire or willingness of someone to do something.* However, when we're looking at a definition of motivation in the workplace, the following describes what we're focusing on:

> A set of forces that <u>*energizes, directs,*</u> and makes people <u>*persist*</u> in their efforts to accomplish a goal.

The reason I selected this definition is because it identifies the "set of forces" that are involved. When we talk about theories of motivation, it's not just one theory acting as a single motivator, rather it's more often a blend of various theories in constantly changing proportions that directs a person's efforts. Additionally, the idea of how persistent a person will be when working to accomplish a goal is also essential. For example, when we use the term *direct*, it means: what are you going to do right now? Are you going to work on the assignment your boss just gave to you, or will you send emails to friends or surf the Web for a while? When we consider the term *persist*, it means: how long are you going to work on it? For five minutes or five hours? What are the forces that are in play here? That's exactly what we're going to cover in the next chapter.

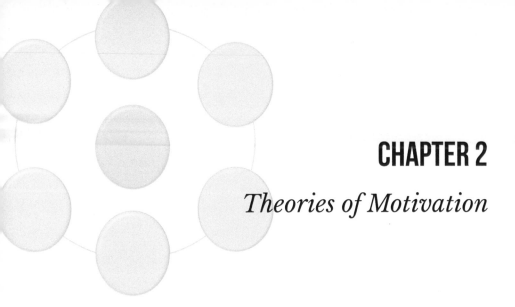

CHAPTER 2

Theories of Motivation

O ften as supervisors or managers, we may say an employee isn't motivated. But what that may really mean is the employee isn't motivated in the direction we desire. The employee may be expending considerable energy—but it may be their energy is directed toward other things. This is where understanding the Theories of Motivation becomes essential.

There are six main Theories of Motivation:

1. Expectancy Theory
2. Needs Theory
3. Outcomes Theory, also known as Two-Factor Theory
4. Goal-Setting Theory
5. Equity Theory
6. Psychological Empowerment

I created the concept of a Ring of Motivation, depicted in Figure 2.1, which illustrates that motivation is not just one singular element but is rather a set of distinct forces that constantly interact in varying proportions. Some of those forces may be internal to the employee, such as self-confidence, whereas other forces are external to the employee, such as the goals an employee is given.

Figure 2.1 Ring of Motivation

We can further divide these motivation theories into two subcategories: Content Motivation Theories, which explain or predict behavior based upon a person's needs, and Process Motivation Theories, which explain *how* people choose behaviors to fulfill their needs.

The Content Motivation Theories are highlighted in red in Figure 2.2. As mentioned earlier, Outcomes Theory is also known as Two-Factor Theory. For the purposes of this book, the two factors we want to focus on are the expectant outcomes by the employee, and whether those outcomes are intrinsic or extrinsic.

The remainder of the theories illustrated in the circle in Figure 2.2 are categorized as Process Motivation Theories, which explain _how_ people choose behaviors to fulfill their needs.

Figure 2.2 Content Motivation Theories

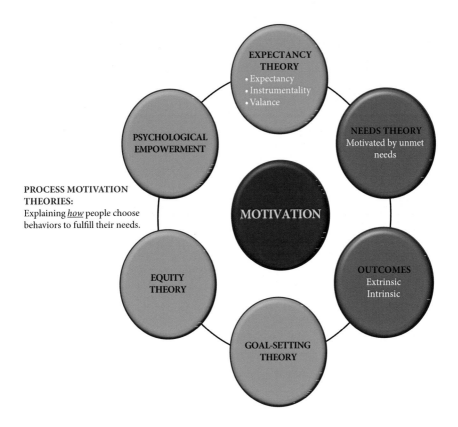

Figure 2.3 Process Motivation Theories

The Process Motivation Theories are highlighted in green in Figure 2.3. As we look at this Ring of Motivation, let's begin our discussion of these theories at the top of the ring beginning with Expectancy Theory.

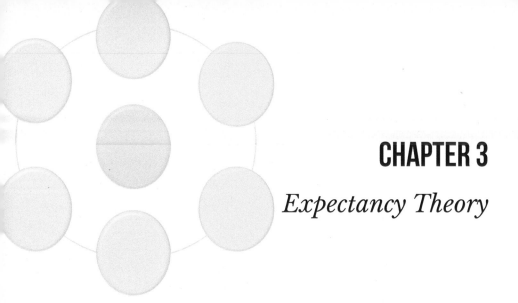

CHAPTER 3

Expectancy Theory

Expectancy Theory is probably the most difficult theory to understand initially, perhaps because researchers have assigned the equivalent of a mathematical formula to it, and the explanation can seem very academic. While the explanation may seem academic, it's essential to understand the concept behind the theory. Please bear with me as I walk you through this critical formula. This might seem dry and boring for a moment, but it will get better shortly.

The mathematical formula researchers have assigned to Expectancy Theory is:

$$M = E \times I \times V$$

The following list defines the variables in the equation:

- M = Motivation
- E = Expectancy
- I = Instrumentality
- V = Valance

Expectancy is the belief that a high level of EFFORT leads to a specific level of PERFORMANCE. $E \rightarrow P$

Instrumentality is the belief that successful PERFORMANCE will bring a specific level of OUTCOMES. P → O

Valance is the anticipated value of the OUTCOMES associated with PERFORMANCE, i.e., the performance results in something meaningful to the contributor, V

So, what do these terms mean in real life? Let's begin with Expectancy. **Expectancy** represents the belief that exerting a **high level of effort** will result in the successful performance of some task.

Think of a task you're not particularly good at, such as writing romantic poetry. You may not be very motivated to write romantic poetry because you believe your effort, <u>no matter how hard you try</u>, will NOT result in a poem that "moves" your significant other.

One of the most critical factors that shapes our expectancy for a particular task is self-efficacy—<u>the belief that we have the capabilities needed</u> to execute the behaviors required to succeed. If we believe we don't possess the skills or abilities necessary to execute the task, any performance we attempt will be lacking because we doubt our abilities. Subsequently, this lackluster performance prevents us from ever considering the outcome stage. If we never get to the outcome, it doesn't matter if the outcome has any valance to us because we never give it any consideration one way or the other.

Now, let's assume we *are* confident that we have the knowledge, skills, and ability to successfully perform the given task. The next question is: Will the outcome have valance to me?

Back when I was in high school, my needs were simple because my parents supplied the majority of my basic needs. My parents put a roof over my head, put clothes on my body, and food on the table. All I needed at the time was enough money to pay for my car insurance, put gasoline in the gas tank, and have enough left over to take my girlfriend out on a date occasionally. I didn't need much. If I got a job at the local burger stand flipping burgers and mixing milkshakes, that's all I needed. Minimum wage and 25-hours per week fit my school schedule perfectly. I had the skills to flip those burgers and mix those shakes, and the outcome had absolute value to me because it fulfilled all of my needs at the time.

Decades later, as an adult, I still have the eye–hand coordination to flip those burgers and skillfully mix a milkshake. So, I know I can still do the job. But at 25-hours per week, with minimum wage and no benefits for my family, even though I can physically still do the job, it doesn't fulfill the needs I have as an adult. Therefore, even with skillful performance, the outcome has no valance to me.

According to Expectancy Theory, the direction of effort is dictated by three beliefs:

- EXPECTANCY (E→P)
- INSTRUMENTALITY (P→O)
- VALANCE (V)

Here's where the mathematical formula comes into this explanation.

$$\text{Motivation force} = (E{\rightarrow}P) \times (\Sigma\ (P{\rightarrow}O) \times V)$$

The Sigma symbol (Σ) signifies that instrumentalities and valances are judged with various outcomes in mind, and motivation increases as successful outcomes are linked to more attractive outcomes. Notice this mathematical formula is a multiplication formula. And remember, any number (or factor) multiplied by zero, equals what? Zero! If any one of the variables we just described is zero, then the motivation force will equal zero as well.

There is one last detail we need to understand about Valance, because it will come up again later in this section. Valance can be positive or negative. A positive valance means I prefer having outcome X vs. not having it, i.e., salary increases, bonuses, rewards. A negative valance means I prefer not having outcome X vs. having it, i.e., disciplinary actions, demotions, terminations.

If you have ever watched the *Dr. Phil* show on television, you'll remember that he asks the guests on the stage, "What are you getting out of that? You wouldn't be doing that behavior if you weren't getting something from it!" Dr. Phil was telling people that they are doing the certain behavior to fulfill some need; the question is... what is the need? That's what we're going to discuss next: Needs Theory.

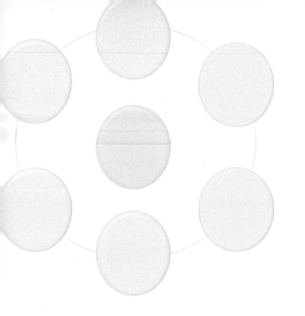

CHAPTER 4

Needs Theory

Needs are the physical or psychological requirements that must be met to ensure human survival and well-being. At the lowest level are our physiological needs, which include food, water, and shelter. Without those, we cannot survive. Without those, we cannot focus on anything else; we must fulfill these most basic needs, otherwise, our every waking thought will be focused on these lowest-level needs until they are fulfilled.

Needs Theory suggests that people are motivated by unmet needs. For example, imagine one morning you skip breakfast, work hard all morning long, and continue working through your lunch break. Even though you may be committed to the work you're doing, at some point, the unsatisfied need of hunger will create enough internal tension and your focus will shift to satisfying that unmet need. This is the basic premise of Maslow's Hierarchy of Needs.

When I was first introduced to Maslow's Hierarchy of Needs, the concept went right over my head. Years later, it finally made sense to me and I understood how it relates to the workplace. Maslow established a five-tier model of human needs where the needs at the lower level must be satisfied before any higher-level need can be fulfilled. If a person achieves a higher-order need and suddenly a lower-order need is unsatisfied, the attention will return to the lower-order need until it is once again fulfilled. Figure 4.1 depicts the five tiers, which we will revisit in a moment.

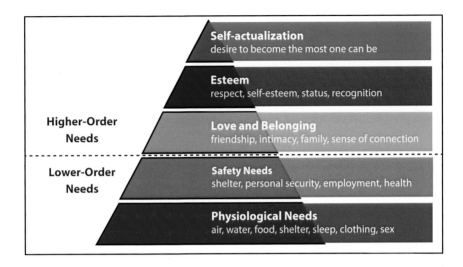

Figure 4.1 Maslow's Hierarchy of Needs

Although psychologist Clayton Alderfer condensed Maslow's five tiers into three tiers, Existence, Relatedness, and Growth (ERG), he has a very similar concept in regard to human needs. Figure 4.2 illustrates how Alderfer categorizes them and names them differently. Primarily, Alderfer's categories are similar in nature—he merged a couple of Maslow's tiers and renamed them, however, they represent the same ideas.

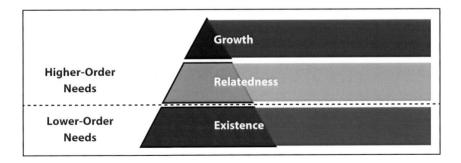

Figure 4.2 Alderfer's Needs Theory

Psychologist David McClelland's Learned Needs Theory proposed the idea that humans have varying needs for power, achievement, and affiliation, as shown in Figure 4.3. McClelland suggests that employees will have a dominant trait they aspire to fulfill. When a supervisor recognizes which dominant trait exists within an employee, they can then make work assignments that fulfill that need, which results in a more productive and happier employee.

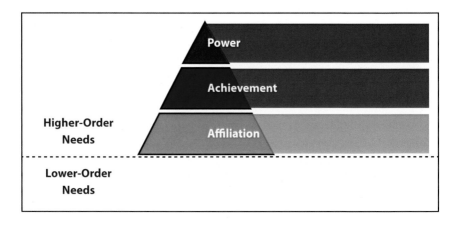

Figure 4.3 McClelland's Learned Needs

In the workplace, I believe a basic understanding of Maslow's Hierarchy of Needs will serve a supervisor or manager well. As shown in Figure 4.4, at the foundational level, the **Physiological Needs** are those we mentioned earlier, which are the basic requirements for human survival: food, water, clothing, shelter, sex, and sleep. Without fulfilling these needs, the human body cannot survive, and everything else becomes secondary until these basic needs are met.

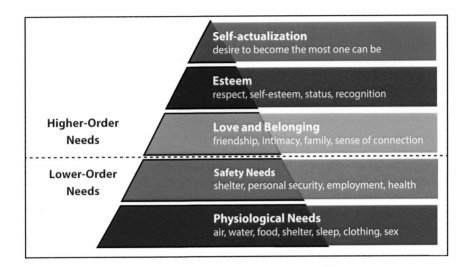

Figure 4.4 Maslow's Hierarchy of Needs (Revisited)

The Need for Safety. These needs align with shelter and protection from the elements as well as security, which means living in a civilized society where there is order and freedom from fear of injury or assault.

The Need for Belongingness. Now we cross the threshold to the higher-order needs that are more social in context. These include friendship, intimacy, trust, and being part of a group, whether that's family, friends, or work.

The Need for Esteem. Maslow divided this level into two categories:

1. the regard for oneself, i.e., dignity, achievement, independence, and
2. the desire for respect from others, i.e., status and prestige.

The Need for Self-Actualization. This occurs when a person has achieved personal success, they are at the peak of their abilities, and they have become all they can become or aspire to become. This is the pinnacle of personal success.[2]

Now take a moment and think of your employees and where they may be on Maslow's hierarchy. Let's picture one of your stronger employees at the high-end of the Esteem level. Everyone highly respects them, and they do a fantastic job in your organization. This person is one of your most influential informal leaders and is a role model for all other employees. Imagine one day that high performing employee comes to you and tells you their spouse filed for divorce, and they are about to lose their home and custody of their children. What need is that employee now focused on?

This is where Maslow's Hierarchy of Needs makes sense in the workplace. Perhaps it's not a divorce, but other life events that will cause your employees to move up and down this hierarchical list. Understanding this concept can help you not only empathize with your employees but also understand the physiological changes they are experiencing.

Employee Engagement and Needs Theory

One of the topics that often comes up in my classes is the concept of employee engagement.

Employee engagement means that workers:[3]

- Have a strong emotional bond to their organization,
- Are actively involved in and committed to their work,
- Feel their jobs are important, and
- Know their opinions and ideas have value.

---

2   Maslow, A. H. "A Theory of Human Motivation." Psychological Review, vol. 50, no. 4, 1943, pp. 370–96.
3   Evans, James R. Quality & Performance Excellence: Management, Organization and Strategy, 5th ed. (Mason, OH: Thomson Business and Economics, 2008).

Needs Theory is closely tied to employee engagement and is rooted in the psychology of Maslow's Hierarchy of Needs. Employees who have advanced upward into the higher-order levels of human needs desire work that is exciting; they desire to assume more responsibility and garner more recognition for their efforts. These higher-level job responsibilities, or engagement, provide a powerful means of fulfilling those higher-level human needs of self-actualization and fulfillment as described by Maslow.

Next, we'll discuss the rewards employees receive as a result of their work and how that relates to Outcomes Theory.

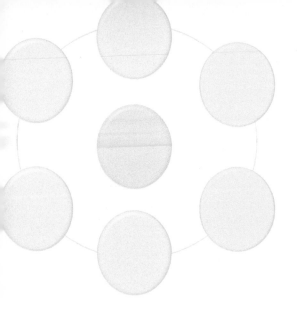

CHAPTER 5

Outcomes Theory

Instead of Outcomes Theory, this should probably be called Rewards Theory because that's what we're really talking about in this section. The "rewards" in exchange for some sort of performance. These rewards are divided into two categories: extrinsic and intrinsic rewards.

Extrinsic outcomes (rewards) are tangible and visible to others and are given to employees on the basis of performance related to specific tasks or behaviors. Intrinsic outcomes (rewards) are the natural rewards associated with performing a task or activity for its own sake. Some examples of intrinsic rewards include:

- A sense of accomplishment or achievement
- A feeling of responsibility
- The chance to learn something new or interact with others
- The fun that comes from performing an interesting, challenging, and engaging task.

Figure 5.1 shows a Facebook post from a friend of mine. After I saw this post on Facebook, I asked for her permission to use this post in my classes to illustrate the concept of motivation.

The young woman in this post is an animal control officer for a small city outside of Seattle, Washington. When you read this post, you will notice that she begins the post by describing the reasons "why" she is an animal control officer. You can feel her passion for this type of work in her post. Even though you can sense her passion, consider the fact that her position as an animal control officer is not among the highest-paid positions in her organization, and it doesn't have any real career path. So why is she so passionate about her work? Basing your opinion on what she wrote in the post, is her primary motivator the size of her salary or getting the next promotion? Obviously not. After reading what she wrote, would you say this is an example of extrinsic or intrinsic motivation?

Figure 5.1 Intrinsic or Extrinsic Motivation?

Content of the post:

> *Why do I do what I do? Animals can't speak for themselves. Sure,*
> *they can bark, yelp, whimper and whine. But can they really speak*
> *for themselves in situations where they are mistreated, and tell you*
> *what's right or wrong? No. That's my job. So many animals don't*

get a fair chance at life. They don't get treated fairly and they don't get a choice. I love animals and I always have, since I was a little girl with hamsters and cats begging my mom for more. Bartering with her on stipulations to get the next parrot (Syriss) or "foster fail cat" (Samson).

Spending every paycheck on them. The ONLY time I EVER asked my parents to borrow money was for vet bills for my pets. Animals are my life, and my career. They are so innocent and kind. They don't know right from wrong and they could never do the harm that the human race is capable of. That is why I do what I do.

This is clearly an example of intrinsic motivation. This young woman loves her work and is a perfect fit for the position of Animal Control Officer. Because of this intrinsic motivation, she works very hard, is well-respected by her coworkers, and has very positive interactions with the community. This young woman doesn't come to work for the paycheck; she comes to work because she is inspired by what she considers to be meaningful work. This work connects with her heart and soul.

Studies that have been conducted over the last several decades have shown that while employees need a paycheck to put a roof over their heads and feed their families, they are motivated much more by meaningful and important work. When employees feel a connection to important and meaningful work, the paycheck is merely a secondary reason they come to work.

Figure 5.2 lists examples of extrinsic outcomes (rewards) and intrinsic outcomes (rewards).

Notice that each list of outcomes also has a "negative" valance, i.e., I would prefer to avoid disciplinary actions, or demotions, or termination. In the intrinsic list, the negative valance is avoiding boredom, anxiety, or frustration.

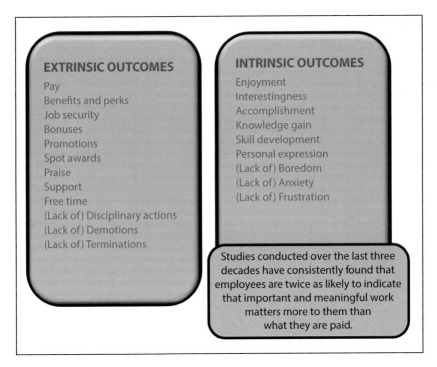

EXTRINSIC OUTCOMES

Pay
Benefits and perks
Job security
Bonuses
Promotions
Spot awards
Praise
Support
Free time
(Lack of) Disciplinary actions
(Lack of) Demotions
(Lack of) Terminations

INTRINSIC OUTCOMES

Enjoyment
Interestingness
Accomplishment
Knowledge gain
Skill development
Personal expression
(Lack of) Boredom
(Lack of) Anxiety
(Lack of) Frustration

Studies conducted over the last three decades have consistently found that employees are twice as likely to indicate that important and meaningful work matters more to them than what they are paid.

Figure 5.2 Extrinsic and Intrinsic Outcomes. (Based on Colquitt, Lepine, Wesson, *Organizational Behavior*, p. 184)

The negative valance of extrinsic outcomes can also be a reliable deterrent to unacceptable behaviors in the workplace. When an employee receives disciplinary action, or a demotion, or is terminated, there is a current debate whether the offending behavior should be publicized in the workplace. The discussion stems around protecting the employee's privacy vs. illustrating the unwanted behavior and the nexus to the negative valance. There is certainly value in employees learning that behavior "X" will result in termination, and if they don't want to be terminated, they'll certainly avoid behavior "X." At the same time, depending upon the circumstances, there is value in treating the employee with dignity and respect and not publicizing the behavior that resulted in termination. You will have to evaluate the given circumstances in your own workplace, and perhaps consult with your legal counsel to determine which course of action you will take.

CHAPTER 6

Goal-Setting Theory

G oal-Setting Theory views goals as the primary drivers of the intensity and persistence of effort. Accordingly, specific and difficult goals will result in higher levels of performance than:

- Assigning no goals
- Assigning easy goals, or
- Assigning "Do your best" goals

As an example, let's say your boss just gave you an assignment. You feel confident you can perform well on the assignment, and you also believe successful performance will result in an outcome that has value to you. (In this case, as stated in Expectancy Theory, we have Expectancy, Instrumentality, and Valance.) Now that you've chosen to direct your efforts to this new assignment, two critical questions remain:

1. How hard will you work on this assignment?
2. How long will you work on this assignment?

In order to gain some clarity, you ask your boss, "So, exactly when do you need this done?"

She thinks for a moment and says, "Just do your best."

Now you return to your desk with the same self-efficacy, instrumentality, and valance as before, but you're still not sure how much you should focus on this new assignment or how long you should work on it before turning to something else. This is a clear example of a "do your best" goal. In this case, there is a clear void of anything driving the intensity of effort. Whereas, if the boss's response had been, "Have the assignment on my desk by 10:30 am Tuesday, with absolutely no mistakes." You'd know exactly how hard to work and for how long.

The basic premise of Goal-Setting Theory is the belief that people will be motivated to the extent they accept specific, challenging goals and receive feedback indicating their progress toward achieving them. You can imagine as a supervisor if you assign a task or goal to someone who doesn't believe they have the knowledge, skills, or ability to complete the task or goal (lack of self-efficacy), they may not speak up and voice their concerns at the moment you give them the assignment. Instead, they may walk away, thinking silently to themselves, "there is a significant disconnect between you and reality." Beyond having a newfound lack of respect for you as their boss, they are now stressed because they know they are on a path to failure with this new assignment. It is essential to have an environment of trust where open and candid conversation can occur so that you can ask the employee how confident they feel in their ability to perform the new assignment and receive an open and honest answer.

Employees are far more likely to exert a high level of effort to accomplish a task or goal when:

- They have a high level of self-confidence in their abilities to accomplish the task, (including stretch goals), and
- They believe they have the support and potential assistance/coaching from you should they need your assistance in order to succeed.

Simultaneously, the employee needs performance feedback as they progress toward accomplishing the goal. If a goal is set during an annual performance appraisal and you wait until the next annual performance appraisal to ask, "How'd you do on that goal we set last year?" That is <u>not</u> performance feedback!

Imagine if you were playing a video game with the intent of beating a friend's score, yet you couldn't see your own score (no feedback on performance) how would you know how hard to try?

There are four basic components that are related to successfully applying Goal-Setting Theory.

- <u>Goal specificity</u>—is the extent to which goals are detailed, exact, and unambiguous.
- <u>Goal difficulty</u>—is the extent to which a goal is difficult or challenging to accomplish.
- <u>Goal acceptance</u>—is the extent to which people consciously understand and agree to the goal(s).
- <u>Performance feedback</u>—is information about the quality or quantity of past performance that indicates whether progress is being made toward the accomplishment of a goal(s).

To successfully create and assign goals, all four criteria must be present.

CHAPTER 7

Equity Theory

E quity Theory considers that motivation doesn't just depend on your own beliefs and circumstances; it also depends on what happens to other people. Remember that assignment your boss gave you that is due at 10:30 am on Tuesday with zero mistakes? Of course, you do because you have been working on nothing else except that assignment. You have been so focused on this assignment you haven't even taken time to refill your coffee cup. Then the guy from across the hall pops his head into your office, and you tell him about the assignment you're working on. He nods sympathetically, saying, "Yeah, the boss gave me a similar assignment that sounds just as tough. I think she realized how tough it was though because she said I could use the company's playoff tickets if I finished it on time."

What? The guy across the hall is getting playoff tickets for finishing his project on time? Playoff tickets weren't offered to me. Well, why am I working so hard? Maybe it's time I take a break and refill my coffee cup if that's the lack of consideration I'm getting for working so hard.

Equity Theory doesn't depend just on your own beliefs and circumstances, but also on what happens to other people.

In my professional life, I have seen Equity Theory destroy the morale of an organization faster than anything else. Equity Theory suggests that everyone is continuously comparing their ratio of inputs and outcomes to the ratio of some "comparison other." In essence, everyone is continuously engaged in a sort of cognitive calculus. There are three results that can arise from this type of cognitive calculus:

- Balanced—the ratio of your inputs and outcomes is fair or equal between you and your "comparison other."
- Under reward—your ratio of inputs and outcomes is less than your "comparison other." (Equity Distress)
- Over reward—Your ratio of inputs and outcomes is more than your "comparison other." This results in not only Equity Distress, but also in guilt and anxiety because you recognize you're getting more than your "comparison other."

The interesting aspect about Equity Theory is that it is not a learned behavior, but rather it's in our DNA. It's a primal reaction to experiencing unequal or unfair treatment. There is a TED Talk featuring Frans de Waal speaking about Moral Behavior in Animals. This 16-minute video is easy to find on YouTube. There is also a 3-minute excerpt from that TED Talk that can also be found on YouTube. While the video is humorous to watch, it also illustrates that animals of all sorts (dogs, birds, chimpanzees) recognize inequity. In the video, two monkeys have been taught to perform a specific task. When the monkeys do the task, they get a food reward. Frans de Waal explains the monkeys love pieces of cucumber as a food reward and will perform the assigned task repeatedly in exchange for a cucumber reward. However, the monkeys prefer grapes as a food reward, and among the monkeys, a grape is considered a much more valuable food reward.

In the video, you can see the first monkey do the task and receive a piece of cucumber as the food reward and is perfectly happy with the cucumber. The second monkey performs the task but instead of a piece of cucumber, gets a grape as a food reward. The first monkey sees the second monkey get a grape and almost seems excited to perform the task again, thinking the reward has now been elevated to grapes. So, the first monkey does the task again, but instead of getting the expected grape, she gets a piece of cucumber as the food reward. The first monkey does not eat the second piece of cucumber, but instead reaches outside the enclosure and throws the cucumber back at the trainer. The first monkey then starts banging her hand on the countertop and begins shaking the enclosure as though she's demanding to also receive a grape. The second monkey performs the same task again, and again gets a grape as a food reward. Now the first monkey is getting extremely excited because she's sure there's got to be a grape in her future this time. But lo and behold, she does the task a third time, and again she gets a piece of cucumber. And just like before, she reaches outside the enclosure and throws it back at the trainer. This experiment demonstrates that the recognition of inequity is not a learned behavior but is a primal instinct in all of us.

16-minute version: https://youtu.be/GcJxRqTs5nk

3-minute excerpt: https://youtu.be/meiU6TxysCg

When employees perceive inequity, there are a variety of ways they may respond to attempt to restore equity. They may decrease or withhold their inputs, i.e., put less effort into their work. They may try increasing their outcomes by asking for a raise. Or they may approach their boss and ask them to correct the imbalance. They may also go to their union, or Federal agencies, or may even file a case in court.

For example, in 2001, employees of the Family Dollar Store sued the company claiming the company had misclassified hourly employees (who are eligible for overtime pay) as managers (who are not eligible for overtime pay). The employees saw this action by the company as an inequity because they believed they were entitled to overtime pay as hourly employees. In 2009, the case was finally settled, and the court ruled that 1,400 employees would divide a $35.6 million judgment against the company ($25,000 each).

Other ways that employees may restore equity is to rationalize or distort inputs and outputs by making mental adjustments, or rationalizing, "… at least I still have a job." And the final way an employee may attempt to restore equity is by changing the "comparison other."

When all other methods to restore equity fail, the employee may decide to quit their job or transfer to another department/division. Or, they may increase their absenteeism by calling in sick more frequently. Supervisors, managers, and executives all need to be alert to the ill effects of Equity Theory at play within the workplace.

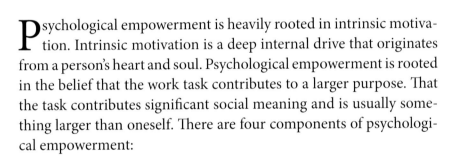

CHAPTER 8

Psychological Empowerment

Psychological empowerment is heavily rooted in intrinsic motivation. Intrinsic motivation is a deep internal drive that originates from a person's heart and soul. Psychological empowerment is rooted in the belief that the work task contributes to a larger purpose. That the task contributes significant social meaning and is usually something larger than oneself. There are four components of psychological empowerment:

- <u>Meaningful</u>—it captures the value of a work goal or purpose, relative to a person's own ideals and passions.
- <u>Self-determination</u>—it reflects a sense of choice in the initiation and continuation of work tasks. Employees can choose how to structure tasks, how long to pursue those tasks, etc.
- <u>Competence</u>—self-efficacy, the ability to do the task.
- <u>Impact</u>—the sense that the actions "make a difference."

Within the component of Competence, the idea of self-efficacy is where supervisors, managers, and executives can have a great deal of influence. For those of you who played sports in school, you can think back to the pep talks your coach would give the team, or to individuals. Those pep talks were meant to boost your sense of self-efficacy and the belief that "you can do this." In the workplace, you can have similar discussions with your employees. When you convey that you have faith in their abilities, faith in their judgment, and that you have all the confidence in the world they can succeed at this task, they are more likely to forge ahead with a stronger sense of self-efficacy. They will also have a higher statistical probability of succeeding because of the psychological empowerment you just gave them. Getting people to believe in themselves is a huge part of psychological empowerment.

The other major components of Competence are *Meaningful* and *Impactful*. These concepts are also important to understand because we will revisit them later when we discuss the importance of an organizational vision statement. As we saw earlier, people are motivated by important, meaningful work. They are inspired by contributing to something larger than themselves. As an organizational leader, it is your responsibility to share this vision with the entire organization.

Simon Sinek wrote a book titled, "*Start with Why: How Great Leaders Inspire Everyone to Take Action.*" He also presented a TED Talk regarding the content of his book that can easily be found on YouTube. The point Sinek makes is that many of us have lost sight of "why" we are in business. If you say you are in business to make a profit, both Sinek and I disagree with you. Profit is a result of doing the thing you do and doing it very well. Why did you start a business to begin with? If you're a non-profit, why did your non-profit organize? Why was it important to create your organization? You started your organization with a particular belief about *why* you were in business. When you can make that "why" the guiding purpose of your business, people who believe what you believe and believe in what you're trying to accomplish, will get on board and be motivated by contributing to something meaningful and larger than themselves.

Once I went into a Tesla car dealership. The thing that struck me most about my visit that day was the fact that I spoke to three different salespeople during my visit, and they all knew the Tesla mission statement. A mission statement is a public declaration of why your organization exists as an organization. But more important than just knowing the mission statement, I could tell that each salesperson was inspired by and believed in the mission. I found this to be an interesting scenario because, in my mind, I was merely shopping in a car dealership. But I soon learned this was not just any car dealership. Tesla's mission statement is to "accelerate the world's transition to sustainable energy." In the minds of the employees with whom I spoke, that's precisely what they were doing, and they were inspired to get it done. Even with my experience studying organizational leadership, I was genuinely amazed to see how inspired these employees were by the mission of their organization—the "why" the organization exists.

Losing track of the "why" your organization exists can also adversely impact your recruitment efforts. If you lose track of the "why" your organization exists, and as a result, within your recruitment efforts advertise inaccurate aspects of the position you are hiring for, you will likely attract applicants who have inaccurate expectations about your organization. Consequently, your newly hired employee may quickly become disillusioned and decide this job is not what they signed up for. I spent 34 years in law enforcement. When I taught my leadership classes at the police academy, I frequently heard complaints from middle-managers and executives about millennials coming into the workforce. A frequent complaint I heard was how impatient millennials were; they didn't want to "pay their dues" and wanted to know when they could get specialty assignments such as SWAT, Detectives, or Crime Scene Investigator. And reportedly, the millennials were asking for these assignments before they were even off probation!

In response to these complaints, I started showing police recruitment videos to my students. Some of these videos were of the highest production quality; some looked like a Hollywood movie. Then I'd ask the students what they had just seen in the recruitment video, what images stuck in their mind? In all of these recruitment videos, the content was heavily weighted with images of SWAT, motorcycles, bicycle patrol, CSI, and all the cool things that law enforcement does. There was very little content about the community or interacting with the community. I'd then ask the students if the recruits might be requesting specialty assignments because that was the sales pitch they were given when they had signed up (via the recruitment video)? Perhaps the recruitment video had lost track of what the law enforcement industry is all about, i.e., the "why" they exist.

Next, I show a recruitment video from the Sioux Falls, South Dakota police department. Nearly the entire content of this video is about the police department interacting with the community and what a wonderful lifestyle there is in Sioux Falls. Yes, there was a little bit of SWAT, and a little bit of CSI, but the overall emphasis was not on these aspects. Instead, the video was heavily weighted in community. The video was so well done, that even this 34-year law enforcement professional considered moving to Sioux Falls! The point I make to the class is that the Sioux Falls recruitment video remembers the "why" their organization exists. I'm sure applicants who apply to the Sioux Falls police department have clear expectations of what to expect as an officer in that organization, and probably won't hear any complaints about millennials being impatient for specialty assignments.

Sioux Falls Recruitment Video: https://youtu.be/aqO1GDkKLOY

As an additional contrast on this topic, I also show a recruitment video from Apple. In that video you hear phrases like this:

"The reason you are here, the reason you were hired is because you are at the top of your field, or you have the potential to be at the top of your field."

The video continues by describing a work environment where employees are pushing the envelope to not just be better than the competition, but instead are striving to make products that are the best they can possibly be. The video also describes employees who are unstoppable problem-solvers and who know there's more than one solution to any problem.

The following two quotes from Apple's recruitment video really describe a work environment that is consistent with the entire content of this book, and an environment we all should strive to achieve:

"The best part of working at Apple is actually the feeling that what you've brought to the table has contributed to something greater than yourself. And in that way, you're changing the world."

"I think what Apple gives the employee is the opportunity to be part of something really, really meaningful."

Statements like these tell potential employees that if you want to be part of something meaningful and contribute to something larger than yourself, Apple is the place for you. And, if you consider yourself one of the best in your industry, Apple is the place for you. All of these statements contribute to psychological empowerment and intrinsic motivation.

When we consider the definition of Motivation as "a set of distinct forces," we now have a better understanding of some of the forces that are in effect, in essence, the varying forces of all of the theories of motivation we just covered:

- Expectancy Theory
- Needs Theory—Maslow's Hierarchy of Needs
- Outcomes Theory, Extrinsic & Intrinsic Outcomes
- Goal-Setting Theory
- Equity Theory
- Psychological Empowerment

As a leader, it is important to remember that the "needs" your employees are attempting to fulfill will change over the course of their careers. How can you keep track of the changes that may occur in your employee's lives? Talk with them! Have regular recurring meetings with them. The annual performance appraisal is not enough. Ask open-ended questions like:

- What parts of your job do you like most/least?
- If you could have any job in this organization, which job would you aspire to?
    o   How can I help you get there? What's your role in that success?

- What motivates you to come to work? To come to work here?
- How do you measure personal success at work?
- How do you know when you've put in a good day's work?

As a leader, always be on the lookout for Equity Theory at play in your workplace. Watch for inequities, even little inequities stifle motivation. In that same category, do you have higher-level employees (i.e., managers, executives) taking special considerations for themselves that lower-level employees are not allowed to do? For example, do the higher-level employees wear a casual style of dress other employees are not allowed to do, like wearing shorts or not wearing the company uniform, or do they take excessively long coffee breaks? Do they engage in endless time-wasting activities? Another example of disparate treatment occurs in situations where a corporate office might offer free lunches or have food catered for meetings but the branch offices of the same company never offer free lunches or catered meetings for their employees.

If you're dealing with a motivation issue, don't fall into the trap of offering more money or promotions to stimulate motivation. Remember, research indicates salary alone doesn't buy much happiness. Any happiness resulting from money in the form of a raise or bonus is only short-term happiness. As mentioned before, studies conducted over the last three decades have consistently found employees are twice as likely to indicate important and meaningful work matters more to them than what they are paid. Remember the last time you got a raise? How long did that feel satisfying? How about the pay raise that came with a promotion? How long did that feel satisfying?

Praise

Praise is not a theory of motivation, however, praise may have as strong an impact on performance as other forms of motivation.

Praise works by boosting levels of dopamine in the brain, which is a chemical linked to joy. As a supervisor or leader, giving praise costs nothing and takes only minutes. However, unearned praise is condescending and destructive, so be sure to only praise good performance.

Additionally, beyond the boost of dopamine, praise is a motivator because it meets the employee's need for esteem and self-actualization (Maslow's Hierarchy of Needs). Praise is probably the most powerful, easiest, and least costly motivational technique there is, and yet it is also the most underutilized.

Be an Advocate

An advocate is one who supports or promotes the interests of another person. Being an advocate is an element of Servant Leadership, i.e., facilitating another's success. When an employee believes you are their advocate and that you have their best interest at heart, you create a connection of trust that enables crucial conversations and constructive feedback to take place, which results in positive behavior changes in the employee.

We've now wrapped up our section on the theories of motivation. To summarize, we have covered how motivation is a "set of forces." We've discussed how people's different needs drive their behavior and we also have a better understanding of how people choose behavior to fulfill their needs. As you can see, no single theory of motivation is individually responsible for employee motivation at any given time. The individual needs of your employees are unique and will continuously change as employees progress through their careers. Accordingly, the tools and theories of motivation you consider and apply will need to be adjusted as the dynamics in your employees' lives change.

This section alone does not give you enough information to answer the question we first started with:

> Do employees bring motivation to the workplace, or does the workplace provide an environment that promotes employee motivation?

One essential part of intrinsic motivation related to the workplace is the purpose or mission of the organization and how meaningful (i.e., meaningful, important work motivates the employee) that purpose or mission is to the individual employee. We'll cover that concept later in this book but before we get to that topic, we're going to talk about systems within the workplace.

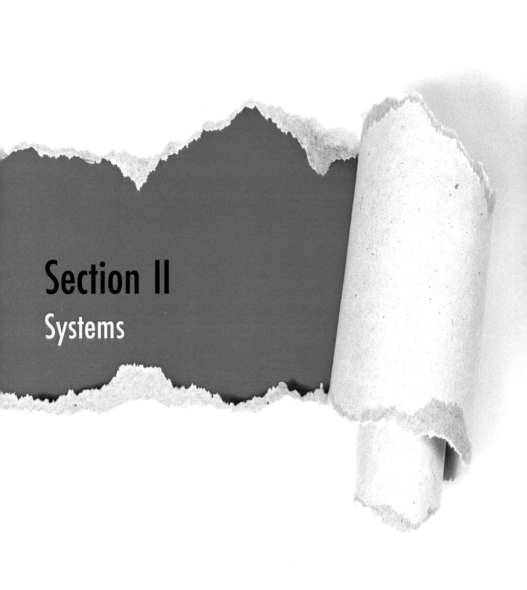

Section II
Systems

CHAPTER 9

Recognizing Systems

Virtually everything we do in our organizations is a system. It's a path to get from the starting point, Point A, to the endpoint, Point B. In the majority of instances, it's a system we created ourselves to satisfy some need within our organization or to delineate the step-by-step process/procedure for how we want a work effort to be performed. As a result, the processes your business creates to address certain needs/purposes may be completely different from the processes created by the business next door, which are designed to address the exact same needs. For example, the process your company uses to manage employment applications may be completely different than the process used by the business next door. The processes are different because each process was created internally by each company to satisfy its own needs. Even though the processes are different, every process can be mapped in the form of a flowchart.

Figure 9.1 shows an example of an overly simplified flowchart of a possible system created by an organization to accept and process employment applications. The process starts at Point A by posting the job opening and required qualifications. The applicant then submits an application and resume. The applicant's qualifications are reviewed to determine if they satisfy the company's needs. If the applicant does not possess satisfactory qualifications, their name is added to a list of unsatisfactory applicants. If their qualifications are satisfactory, the applicant's references are checked. A decision is then made whether to schedule the applicant for an interview. If the decision is to not schedule them for an interview, the applicant is notified of that decision. If the decision is to schedule them for an interview, then a date and time for an interview is scheduled. The applicant then attends the interview and is then notified of the hiring decision.

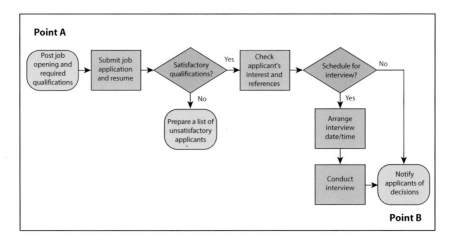

Figure 9.1 A Simplified Flowchart

Figure 9.1 represents a simple example of a flowchart; however, the purpose of the flowchart has two parts. First, it helps to determine if the path from Point A to Point B is as efficient as possible and, second, it helps to determine if the process produces a quality output. Of course, not all processes are as simple as the process illustrated in Figure 9.1.

Figure 9.2 shows a Cross-Functional Process Map, which means the path of the flowchart crosses divisional boundaries within the organization. On the left side of Figure 9.2, the process begins with the Customer, it then moves to the Sales department, then to Production, then to Purchasing, and ends with Customer Service.

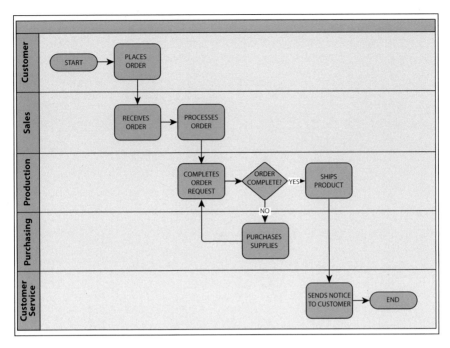

Figure 9.2 A Cross-Functional Process Map

In this case, the process begins with a customer placing an order. The Sales department receives and processes the order by sending it to Production. The Production division is expected to complete the order, but if it can't, Production sends a request to Purchasing to purchase supplies so the order can be completed. Once the supplies are purchased, the order is returned to Production, which completes the order by shipping the order to the customer and sending them a notice that their order has been shipped. Figure 9.2 represents a fictional process that is meant to illustrate the concepts of a cross-functional process map where a process can span multiple divisions within an organization.

In the next chapter we are going to review cross-functional process maps within a real work environment. These upcoming examples will show us the real-life benefits of mapping flowcharts to analyze a system.

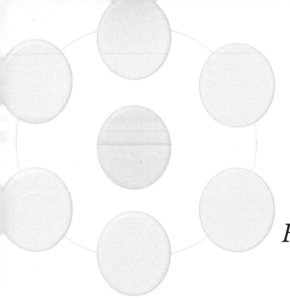

CHAPTER 10

Recognizing the Red Flag Warnings

Other than outright failure, how do you know if there's a problem with a system in your organization? Many times, there are warning signs that go unnoticed until a system finally comes to complete failure. Often those warning signs come in the form of comments or questions from the employees who are closest to that system. Those comments or questions usually have a negative tone:

"This sucks"

"This is stupid" or

"Why do we do this?" or

"Why do we do it this way?"

Historically many organizations responded to these comments with a deaf ear, particularly when an employee would ask, "why do we do this?" Often the answer would be something like, "we've always done it that way," or "just do what we tell you to do." If an employee asks the question, "why do we do this?" and you're unable to articulate a good explanation, that could be a red flag that perhaps this process needs some attention. The following is an example from a police department.

A new police officer was working with their training officer. The pair had just finished handling a domestic violence call, and the student officer was writing the resultant report and completing the department-required forms for this type of call. The student officer held up one of the department-required forms and asked the training officer, "Why do we fill out this form?" Historically, many training officers may have responded by saying, "I don't know, we've done it this way for years, just do what we tell you and quit asking so many questions." Fortunately, in this case, the training officer was more enlightened and responded with, "I don't know; let me find out."

The training officer went to the sergeant and inquired about the form. The sergeant didn't know the answer either. Then the sergeant went to the Records section and asked the records clerk why this form was necessary. The records clerk said she didn't know either. The sergeant asked, "What do you do with these forms when you receive them? The clerk replied, "We file them in the bottom drawer over there in that filing cabinet," as she pointed toward a filing cabinet located on the other side of the room.

Now let's hit the pause button on this story for a moment. We've now encountered four employees who don't know why the form is being completed on every domestic violence case. The next step in this research project is on the far side of the room—the bottom drawer of the filing cabinet. Because we're talking about systems in this section, are we beginning to see a trend developing? What will we find in the mysterious bottom drawer? Will a clown pop out of the drawer like a jack-in-the-box holding a note with the answer we seek? Perhaps a magic genie will emerge from a puff of smoke holding that answer. What do you think the sergeant will find in this mystical drawer? Let's hit the play button and resume the story.

The sergeant walked over to the file cabinet. He bent over, grasped the handle, and with his thumb, released the latch. He then slowly opened the bottom drawer to reveal the contents. And POOF! No jack-in-the-box. No magical genie. Instead, the sergeant discovered more than three years' worth of the department-required domestic violence forms.

Upon further research, it was discovered that approximately three years prior, a PhD candidate had been working on their doctoral thesis about domestic violence. The candidate asked the police department if they could collect domestic violence statistics for three months on a form that was created by the candidate. The PhD candidate got their three months' worth of statistics and went on to complete their PhD thesis. However, the police department never stopped completing the forms.

In this example, there are several points where this opportunity to recognize the red flag warning could have failed. First, a fresh set of eyes, i.e., the new officer, asked the original question, "Why do we do this?" What would have happened if no one had ever asked that question? Second, the training officer could have given the old autocratic leadership answer of, "Because I said to do it." Or, "We've always done it this way." Likewise, when the training officer went to the sergeant, the sergeant could have given the same autocratic leadership answer. Fortunately, they were all enlightened enough to realize they didn't know "why," and should do more research. In this case, the form had been completed needlessly for nearly three years. So, the main takeaway is the following: if an employee asks, "Why do we do this?" and you don't have a clear answer or explanation, the lack of an answer is a definite red flag. That red flag indicates you need to do some research to determine if you should even be doing this process in the first place, and if so, why. If your research uncovers a valid "why," then it's important to communicate the "why" to all of your staff, so they will become aware of the validity of the process, be able to share it with others, and be able to make better decisions regarding issues surrounding this process.

Another red flag warning is when your employees tell you a process is "stupid" or "this process doesn't make sense." Remember, the people who perform a given process on a daily basis know it better than anyone—because they do it *every day*. When they begin making comments that are red flag warnings, you will want to pay attention. This next scenario is an example of cost inefficiency, where red flag comments were ignored for years. In a different police department, the executive level added a new service and created a new process where citizens could go online to make a service request, rather than using the usual route of calling the police dispatch center on the phone.

However, instead of these online requests being routed to the Dispatch center, the requests were routed to the deputy chief's email. Occasionally, the deputy chief would make a telephone call to the person making the request, sometimes to find out more information, and sometimes to give the appearance of responsive customer service. From here, the deputy chief would forward the online request to a patrol captain. Usually, the captain would call the Dispatch center on the phone and inform them he was emailing an online service request to them and ask them to enter the request into the computer-aided dispatch system as a call for service and then dispatch the event as appropriate. However, one bottleneck in the system would occur when the deputy chief forwarded the service request to the captain's email. Sometimes, the captain was away at training or gone for vacation. As a result, the request could sit in the email inbox for several days before receiving any attention, which qualifies as poor customer service.

Once the online request was forwarded to the Dispatch center, it was handled just like any other call for service, with one exception. Occasionally, a week or two after the original incoming request, particularly if the deputy chief had previously made a phone call to the person making the online request, the deputy chief would ask the captain about the resolution of that incident. The captain would then have to research the outcome of that incident and report back to the deputy chief.

This process continued for several years. During the entire time, the two captains assigned to Operations complained that the system was flawed, inefficient, and needed to be redesigned. Yet their complaints fell on deaf ears for years. The captain's primary argument was this: Dispatchers are trained to triage incoming calls for service and dispatch the appropriate resource to respond to the specific request. The captains furthered their case by posing the following question: Just because a call for service comes to the department via a different medium (i.e., online rather than through a telephone call), why was it being routed differently than a phone call? It's still a request for service and should be triaged and handled by the people who are trained for that function. This would also be a more efficient use of taxpayer money because the work would be completed by people specifically trained to do the task (and also at a much lower cost than a deputy chief's wages). Figure 10.1 illustrates the online service request process.

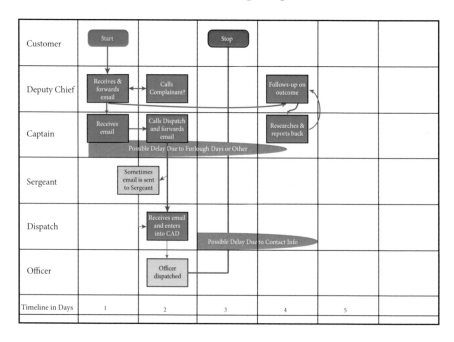

Figure 10.1 Overview of the Online Service Request Process

For years the captains' arguments fell on deaf ears. Some staffers in the chief's office accused the captains of trying to put more work onto the dispatchers, even though

1. this is the task dispatchers are trained and paid to do.
2. the dispatchers were already in the process loop, so it wouldn't be additional work for the dispatchers; improving the process would merely bring dispatchers into the loop earlier.

After being ignored for so long, the captains finally created a flowchart to illustrate the inefficiency of the process for handling on-line service requests, however, they took it one step further. With a little research, they were able to calculate the average amount of time spent on each request and added a column that showed the salary costs of the person performing each specific step (see Figure 10.2).

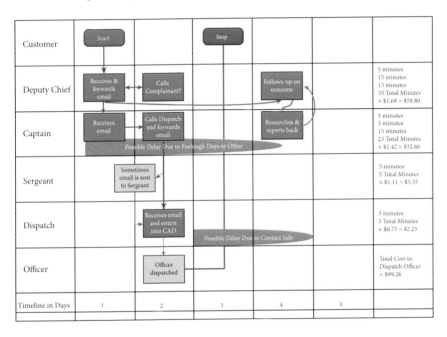

Figure 10.2 Per-Minute Costs Highlighting
Inefficiencies in the Process

Figure 10.2 illustrates the actual cost of the process based on each person's salary. We can see in the deputy chief's row that an average of 5 minutes is spent in the initial review of the request. 15 minutes are spent engaged in a phone call with the person making the request and an additional 15 minutes are spent asking for follow up about the outcome, as well as receiving and reviewing the report on the outcome. On average, each event was consuming 35 minutes of the deputy chief's time at a rate of $1.68 per minute, for a total average cost of $58.80 per request.

Likewise, in the captain's row, you can see the similar activities listed for a sum of 23 minutes at $1.42 per minute for a total average cost of $32.66 per event. As we move to the bottom of the cost column, we can see the total cost to the taxpayers is $99.26 per event.

The captains then submitted a flowchart (Figure 10.3) that detailed the costs associated with an online service request, if the request were routed to the Dispatch center in the same way as an incoming phone call for service.

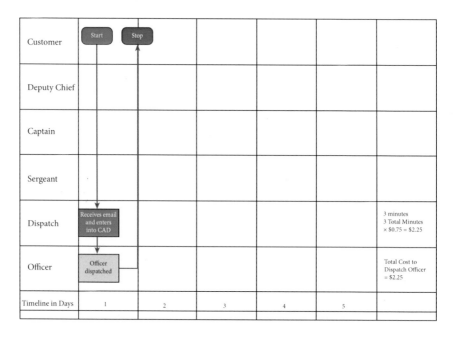

Figure 10.3 Potential Cost Savings of Altering the
Online Service Request Process

A comparison of the two flowcharts revealed the significant cost benefits that could be achieved by improving/altering the process. As we can see in Figure 10.3, the costs dropped from $99.26 to $2.25 per event. The new process would also create more efficiency and better customer service because the service request would be handled on the same day that it was submitted. Once these processes were mapped out in flowcharts such as these, with the average costs highlighted, the executives finally understood what the captains had been complaining about for years, and the process was modified.

The point here is the same as what General Jim Mattis said in his book, *Call Sign Chaos,*

> *It's easy to get into a bureaucratic rut where things are done a certain way because they're done a certain way. That seems absurd when you read it in print—but it's the norm in large organizations. Every few months, a leader has to step back and question what he and his organization are doing.*

Additionally, a leader has to keep their eyes and ears open to the red flag warnings from their followers and be willing to analyze the process. When the person responsible for reviewing the effectiveness of a process is also the same person who created the system, the real challenge is to be disciplined enough to perform a critical review in order to find areas for improvement.

In my classes, we do an exercise to illustrate this point. It's a very simple, and sometimes frustrating, exercise for the students. It illustrates the point that when someone creates a system, they are usually unwilling to change that system until complete system failure occurs. Whereas, if they understand systems and trendlines, they could recognize the red flags that warn that system failure is on the horizon, and corrective action can (and should) be taken before the disaster occurs.

The exercise I use in my classes is called Off the Ground. I have the students stand, and I hand them a piece of paper and refer to the paper as a "mat." Then I put the following instructions on the screen, and from then on, this is the only information they are given. If the students ask a clarifying question, I merely read the instructions out loud as a response to their question.

> *"Your task is for the entire group to simultaneously be up and off the ground for the count of three, using only yourselves and these mats as resources. Being on the mat counts as being off the ground."*

Once the students say they are ready, I count out loud: One... Two... Three! On the count of three, all of the students now have one foot placed on their individual mat, while they skillfully balance on one foot. Mission accomplished.

Now, to simulate changes in the work environment, I take everyone's mat and rip it in half, handing back to them only one-half of the original mat. I then tell them to reread the instructions, and I begin to count: One... Two... Three! This time the students are usually able to complete the task in a very similar fashion to the first effort.

Again, I simulate a change in the work environment by taking everyone's mat, ripping it in half, and handing back to the students only one-half of the mat they just had. I then tell them to read the instructions again, and I begin to count: One... Two... Three! This time the students are still able to complete the task, however, they're usually balancing on the ball of one foot, and either holding hands or grasping their neighbor's shoulder for balancing support.

I continue repeating this process exactly as the previous events. I simulate a change in the work environment by taking everyone's mat, ripping it in half, and handing back to the students one-half of the mat they just had. I repeat the countdown: One... Two... Three! This time the students are able to complete the task, but this time they are usually standing on the tips of their toes, as well as grasping their neighbor's shoulder for balancing support. By now, if the students possessed a "systems" mindset, they'd be able to see the trendline of the changing work environment clearly. They would envision on each successive event the mat is going to continue to be reduced in size by 50%. They would recognize the future of this trend and realize the first solution they came up with in order to accomplish the task, will soon no longer work. The original solution will result in complete system failure, and they will have to develop a new system.

However, the students do not focus on the trendline of the changing environment, and they stick with the original system *they* created until it fails. Now, because of total system failure, they are *forced* to figure out a new system. And because they are being *forced* to find a new solution, it usually doesn't take them very long to create a workable solution. The next time that I count: One... Two... Three! all of the students simultaneously jump into the air, so their feet are off the ground on the count of three. Mission accomplished. However, because the students were so deeply attached to the system they created originally, and because they were not well-versed in *systems* thinking—they ignored the trendline indicating the environment was changing and ignored the clues alerting them that system failure was imminent. It took a complete system failure before any proactive corrective thinking was applied.

Figure 10.4 Systems to the Point of Failure—Necessity is
the Mother of (New Systems) Invention

The "Off the Ground" exercise I use in my classes is very similar to the example of the online service request system mentioned earlier. Because the police department created the system, the creators were very reluctant to change or improve the system. And while the online service request system didn't experience a complete system failure, it was a waste of taxpayer money at nearly $100 per event over several years, which brings us to the topic of types of waste in the workplace.

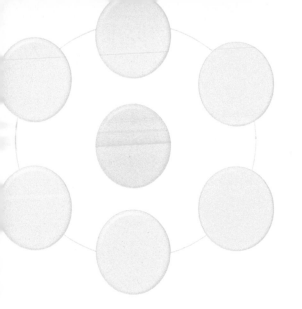

CHAPTER 11

Types of Waste in the Workplace

For years I have used the term *dysfunctional time* to address instances when money is being paid to employees to repeat work they have already been paid for. To better illustrate this concept, I use a fictional example of hiring a contractor to do work on your home. In this example, let's say you hire a contractor to build an additional dwelling unit (ADU) onto your home. The additional dwelling unit will be a one-bedroom, one-bath apartment with a small kitchenette that will be attached to the back of your home. Your intent is to use this ADU as a source of additional rental income for as long as you own this home.

You have the blueprints and building permits in-hand, and you hire a contractor to build the ADU. At the end of the project, you pay the contractor for his work. Now the building inspector arrives, the project does not pass inspection, and the building inspector will not issue a Certificate of Occupancy. Obviously, the contractor did not do his work properly. Now, the question is, are you going to pay the contractor additional money to come back and correct his lousy work? Or, do you expect the contractor to come back and do the job correctly for the amount of money you already paid him? Obviously, you are not going to pay the contractor additional money—you paid the contractor to do a specific job, and you expect him to do the job right.

Yet, in the workplace, we frequently pay employees to correct substandard work. Why do we do that? We already paid the employee for the initial time spent on the first effort—obviously, that was a waste of money because their work product was not acceptable. The time spent by the supervisor to recognize the defect and reject the work product was a waste of time because the outcome we expect to pay for is for a supervisor to review and approve the work product. Now, we are in a position where we are paying the employee to redo their work, and for the supervisor to recheck the work. In essence, we have paid twice for one work product. This is an example of what I refer to as dysfunctional time in the workplace.

There are two points to consider in these examples of dysfunctional time. The first is everyone makes mistakes; it's a fact of life. If someone makes a mistake with the best of intentions while doing their best to carry out your intent, stand by them. The second consideration relates to giving some consideration to the possibility that a system in your organization is contributing to the dysfunctional time. If you provided training on this topic where the employee erred, was the outcome of the training effective? Does the training need to be altered for a better outcome? If you issued a new policy or directive, was the result what you expected, or does the communication process need to be improved? Does the wording of the policy or directive need to be improved in order to more clearly express the intended or expected outcome? In all instances as a leader, as a supervisor, or as a manager, one of your first obligations is to ask yourself the following question:

"What could I have done, or what should I have done, to prevent this from occurring?"

Asking yourself this question will always allow you to be in a better position to analyze your role, your culpability in any problem situation, and to always give your employees the benefit of the doubt. When your employees recognize your pattern of consistently giving them the benefit of the doubt, they will respect and trust you more as a leader.

There may be times when a third option exists. Yes, everyone makes mistakes, but perhaps one individual is making mistakes far more frequently than anyone else. This results in a higher cost of dysfunctional time to the organization than the vast majority of their peers. You should examine your coaching and how well you communicated your intent and analyze if all of your practices are sound. If you're confident your contribution to the process is sound, it is time to delve deeper into the individual employee. Is the employee's intent good, or is the intent malicious? Is the employee distracted with other things going on in their life, i.e., divorce, sick child, dying parent, financial troubles, etc.? Does the employee possess the skills and cognitive ability to perform this task/job? Perhaps this particular job is not a good fit for the employee, and you can help them find a better fit elsewhere in the company, or even in a different company. Of course, if all of this analysis reveals that the employee is either being lazy or malicious, then we must finally turn to corrective actions, mostly through negative valance, which was discussed in the motivation section of this book—but we always want that to be the last course of action.

Another type of waste in the workplace is *idle time*. This is when employees and equipment are not producing value. Examples can include waiting for paperwork, material, or information before they can proceed with their work. Idle time is usually created by a *systems* problem within your organization. If you have idle-time events occurring in the workplace, you need to determine where the bottleneck is within the system and do your best to eliminate it. That bottleneck is costing you money in the form of wasted employee time.

Another form of waste that also leads to poor morale is something I call *workplace hygiene*. Workplace hygiene relates more to the equipment we provide to our employees to do their work efficiently. Unfortunately, this equipment regularly fails, almost to the point of being predictable. For example, recurring events such as when employees go out to the car or truck they need for their route and find that the battery is dead and the car or truck won't start. This often happens because we're trying to eke out as much extended service life from that battery as possible. Or the copy machine that is continually getting a paper jam. Or when an employee submits an electronic report, and the report gets lost or disappears into cyberspace and then must be rewritten. Instances such as these are not only frustrating for the employee but also have a financial cost associated with them in the form of lost productivity.

The last type of waste I will talk about here is work performed by the wrong job classification. An example of this was discussed earlier with the example of the online service request process, where the deputy chief was doing work that should have been assigned to a dispatcher. Work performed by the wrong job classification usually occurs because there is a perception that the person getting the assignment has the capacity in their day to accomplish the task, and it's also believed the job classification that should be assigned the work is already operating at or above capacity. Therefore, there is no capacity to assign this additional work to the lower-paid classification.

In Chapter 10, we looked at a deputy chief who was receiving electronic service requests, when that service request should have been initially routed to a dispatcher. In this example, the work was incorrectly being attended to by someone earning more than $100 per hour, when it should have been assigned to someone earning $45 per hour. If the new additional work exceeds the workload capacity of the dispatcher work unit, it is far more efficient to hire more dispatchers to handle the additional workload, than it is to assign the new work to the wrong job classification and at a higher rate of pay.

All of these types of waste fall under the category of *systems* because they are processes created by the organization, and therefore, can be improved by the organization in order to increase the efficiency of both the organization's human and capital resources. You must be alert to the red flag warnings your employees will give you. You must be alert to the waste of fiscal resources through dysfunctional time, workplace hygiene, or work assigned to the wrong job classification. Equally important, you must be alert to your role, or your culpability, in creating or failing to improve these inefficient systems.

CHAPTER 12

Two Areas Where Organizations Generally Fail

There are two areas where organizations generally fail, and those areas are:

- *Lack of Communication*
- *Lack of Coordination*

When we talk about a lack of communication, there is actually a formula that can be applied to evaluate the effectiveness of communication. It has been said that in instances of the written word alone, such as this book, an email, or a text message—where there is no voice inflection and no body language for the receiver to interpret, only 8% of the intended message is recognized and understood by the receiver. Whereas, if you add voice to the communication process, such as in a telephone call, a podcast, or a radio broadcast, where there is only the spoken word coupled with voice inflection, tone, and pace, just 37% of the intended message is heard by the receiver. Finally, if we analyze a face-to-face interaction where the message includes words, voice inflection, AND body language, 55% of the intended message is heard by the receiver.

- Words = 8% of successful communication
- Tone of Voice = 37% of successful communication
- Body Language = 55% of successful communication

The described percentages differ depending on what resource you may research, but the relative proportions and intent are very similar across all definitions.

Knowing this formula, we must then ask ourselves: What is the most common form of communication we use in our workplace? The answer I hear most often by the students in my classes is email. We recognize that we most often use the least effective method of communication, and then wonder why we have conflict and inefficiency in the workplace.

This is the communication system we have adopted in our workplaces, so we must recognize its limitations and take corrective steps as necessary to improve our communication in the workplace. How often have you sent an email to a coworker whose office or cubicle is only 30-feet away from you when you could have gotten up and walked 30 feet to engage in a more effective face-to-face conversation? Being aware of the efficacy of delivery will vastly improve communication.

Lack of coordination is another area of failure for organizations and can also be a symptom of poor communication. Lack of coordination produces delays that cause inefficiency, and those delays create unreliability and can result in poor customer service. Lack of coordination can also cause duplication of efforts. I am familiar with one instance where two executives discussed a project that needed to be completed within the next week. The project was very labor-intensive and would engage two employees for an entire week in order to complete the project by the deadline. However, due to poor communication and an apparent misunderstanding between the two executives, each executive went to different branches of the organization and assigned different people to work on the same project.

Fortunately, the employees working in the different branches had excellent communication, recognized the mistake, and prevented two different teams from duplicating the work of the other. Had the employees not had a sound system of communication in place, the two teams would have completed the same project independently of each other, which would have resulted in a waste of time and money of two people for an entire week.

CHAPTER 13
Highly Interdependent Systems

In his book, *Leading Change,* John P. Kotter does a lovely job of describing interdependent systems. He uses the example of moving into your new office and wanting to make some changes suitable to your liking. So, you move one chair to the left, put a few of your own books on the credenza, and rehang a painting on the wall. All of these changes take, maybe, an hour of your time. These changes were easy to make because each item was an independent part and could easily be changed or moved. Kotter then adds some complexity to the same issue. He describes a scenario in which you walk into your new office and find an array of ropes, pulleys, bungee cords, and springs connecting different items in the office in what appears to be a haphazard array. As you enter your office, you have to twist and contort your body with the dexterity of a cat to fit between all of these ropes and pulleys as though you are a professional burglar attempting to avoid the laser beam alarm system in a museum.

Once inside the office you decide to move a chair. But this time the chair is very hard to move, and when it finally does move, the bookshelf on an adjacent wall moves also because it's connected to the chair by a rope and pulley. When you move a lamp on the credenza, books fall off the shelf, and your desk chair moves too, because they are all interconnected with ropes and cables. You attempt to move a floor lamp and notice a connecting cable that goes through the wall into the office next to yours. When you move the floor lamp in your office, you discover the floor lamp in the next office has moved too. Now you try to move your desk, and the credenza has moved in a direction you don't like and at the same time your desk lamp is now suspended in mid-air because it's connected to the credenza by a rope going one direction, and a cable that goes in the opposite direction through the wall to some unknown item in the next office.

What Kotter is describing in his book is an example of interconnected systems. Changes to the first office were easy because every item of furniture was independent. When you moved one item, it was the only item affected. However, in the interconnected office, even slight changes had potential impacts on interconnected items, and some of those impacts we either didn't expect, or didn't like the outcome. It was far more challenging to make changes in the second office because of the interconnectivity between the items of furniture.

This example by John P. Kotter serves as a perfect warning to leaders and managers who embark on improving the systems within their organization. First, bravo to you for recognizing your role in making the workplace better but be careful and make sure that you look at the bigger picture because the system you may be changing may have an impact on an interdependent system you didn't anticipate.

Let me give you a real-life example: In early 2018, in the capital city of Washington state, a regional hospital was experiencing challenges with homeless people walking into the emergency room for medical care. Medical care in an emergency room is costly, and to have patients coming in for routine, walk-in care was creating bottlenecks in the ability of the emergency room to operate efficiently. As a solution, the hospital opened a walk-in clinic nearby, where homeless people could walk in for medical care and other services. The new project (or system of delivering medical care), was a huge success. In the emergency room, the number of non-emergency patients decreased significantly, and the new clinic was seeing approximately 200 patients per day. From the hospital's standpoint, this new system of delivering medical services to the community was a success.

The new clinic was so successful that the good word spread among homeless people in other areas, and soon more homeless people from far away began to migrate to the clinic for services. Soon local business owners began to complain that homeless people had taken over the streets and alleys of the city. The business owners claimed they could no longer do business in the city and would be forced to close their stores and move to a different city.

In this example, one system change that appeared to be a success was interconnected to other systems (i.e., the local businesses) and was hurting local businesses and, ultimately, the local economy. Of course, when the hospital executives created their new clinic, they had the best of intentions for the patients they were serving but did not recognize the interconnectivity between their system and the local economy. When you analyze systems within your organization with the intention of improving them and making them more efficient, be sure to include the big picture. You will need to identify whether the system is an easily modified independent system or if there is interconnectivity where changes in one system may adversely impact another system or multiple systems?

CHAPTER 14
The Bottom Line

When we talk about systems in the workplace, the bottom line is this: Virtually everything we do is a system, usually created by us. And because we created the system, we have more faith in the system than is prudent. When analyzing your systems, create a process map or flowchart in order to find efficiencies.

Be alert to red flag warnings. They usually come from our employees in the form of verbal comments such as, "this is stupid," or "why do we do this?" It's easy to get into a rut regarding systems because not only have we created the systems ourselves but they've also been working for so long, and we've become comfortable with the "if it's not broken, don't fix it" mentality. *Don't fall into that trap*! You must be proactive; you must watch for trends that may forecast a system failure is on the horizon. Do not wait for total system failure before you act. Remember, your environment is continually changing, and your systems may need to change with the environment, just like the students in the "Off the Ground" exercise in Chapter 10 had to be responsive to their changing environment.

Look for waste in your workplace. Your efforts will not only save you time and money, but will also result in a workplace with higher employee morale. In all cases, when planning changes and improvements, be alert to interdependent systems, so that the changes you make don't negatively impact someone else.

Section III
Organizational Leadership

CHAPTER 15

Organizational or Executive-Level Leadership

I use the terms *Organizational Leadership* and *Executive-Level Leadership* interchangeably. I'm still trying to figure out which term will be most readily understood, accurately interpreted, and relatable to the work experience of the greatest number of people when they hear the term(s) for the first time. I'm finding that the trend seems to be favoring the term *Organizational Leadership*, which is the reason why I have decided to use it as the title of this section.

Organizational leadership is a different type of leadership than interpersonal leadership. Most leadership books are about interpersonal leadership and are focused on the relationship between the leader and the follower, i.e., the leader–follower dyad. Interpersonal leadership is the type of leadership we are all so familiar with and usually see at lower levels of an organization. It is most commonly seen in first-level supervision or middle-management levels. Don't get me wrong; interpersonal leadership is also crucial at the executive level, but at higher levels in the organization, leaders need to understand and execute organizational leadership skills; otherwise, the organization will flounder if it doesn't fail altogether. Organizational leadership is about providing direction, including the possibility of providing direction to people you may never meet face-to-face. Organizational leadership is about inspiring your employees toward mission accomplishment. It's also about creating an environment where employees are inspired by the direction of the organization. An environment where the employees understand the importance of their role in the big picture and further understand that without their specific role within the organization, mission accomplishment isn't possible. Organizational leadership is the conceptual part of leadership; it's about communicating a vision of the future, and how to make that vision a reality. Creating a vision does not occur at the lower levels of an organization. Creating a vision and implementing a strategy to achieve that vision is what distinguishes organizational leadership from interpersonal leadership. Now, let's step back a moment and apply this model of the conceptual part of leadership to the real world.

In his book, *The E-Myth Revisited*, Michael E. Gerber cites business failure statistics from the Small Business Administration. Gerber says that in the United States, more than 1 million new businesses are created each year. However, by the end of the 5th year, 80% of those businesses will be out of business. Additionally, of the 20% that do survive, by the end of the 10th year, 80% of those will also be out of business. Why do these businesses fail? In his book, Gerber describes a fundamental cause of these failures—and I absolutely agree with his assertion because I have seen it, and I hear about it on an almost daily basis. His assertion is as follows:

People who are great technicians believe they are immediately and eminently qualified to run a business that does that kind of work.

- The handyman opens a business as a homebuilder
- The baker who makes great cupcakes opens a cupcake shop
- The cabinet builder opens a cabinet shop
- The pharmacist opens a drug store

Suddenly, they realize to run a business, being a great technician isn't enough. All at once there are a dozen additional jobs incumbent upon a business owner that they have no idea how to do. Particularly when those new jobs relate to executive-level responsibilities within an organization.

The reason these businesses fail is because of a lack of organizational leadership. The technician-turned-owner fails in the conceptual part of leadership. They fail in vision-creation and direction-setting for the organization because organizational leadership is one of these dozen jobs they don't know how to do because they've only been a technician.

This example relates to what I said in the introduction. I have worked for some very charismatic leaders. They were wonderfully nice people, and early in their careers they were great technicians. But as they moved up the organizational ladder no one ever talked to them about the conceptual part of leadership. Therefore, they failed as leaders, because they weren't leading. They didn't have a vision of a better future for the organization and lacking a vision they didn't have a plan to take the organization anywhere. They were merely along for the ride, most of their time being consumed with trying to keep the ship from sinking.

Being a great technician is ideal for lower levels in the organization. But the skills needed to fulfill the conceptual part of leadership at the executive-level of the organization is a completely different skill set, which is what we're going to talk about next.

CHAPTER 16
Two Components of Leadership

There are two primary components of leadership:

1. **The process of influencing others**. This is the leader–follower dyad I mentioned in the previous chapter. If you've been reading leadership books, you're likely familiar with all of the theories of leadership, ranging from autocratic leadership up to and including participative leadership.

2. **What are you leading toward?** Are you providing "direction" toward the vision, the destination, the end-goal? Are you providing real transformational leadership?

It is this second component (*What are you leading toward*) that is often overlooked in discussions about leadership. In my classes, many students say they want to learn more about leadership. If they are in a middle-management position or higher, I usually reply with a question, "What are you leading toward? The word leadership implies you are "leading" toward something— but what is that *something*?" Nearly 100% of the time the students have no idea how to respond to that question. They have a deer-in-the-headlights reaction—through no fault of their own—because most leadership books don't touch on this concept, and it's very likely this concept has never been mentored or demonstrated in their workplace.

Another question I ask my students is this: Was your organization successful last year? I usually get one or two affirmative responses, but again, the vast majority of students have no idea how to answer this question. I'll add a quick sidebar here to discuss how you might measure success.

If you measure success through bottom-line results, i.e., profit, I strongly disagree with your methodology. Profit is a result of what you **do** and doing it very well. What's the purpose of your organization? What's your cause? What is it that you do? If you **do** that thing, purpose, or cause very well, profit will be a result of that performance.

Henry Ford said profit is essential to business vitality, but a business that charges too much will go out of business just as fast as a business that charges too little. He said smart businesspeople focus on quality and providing a good product or service, and business vitality (i.e., profit) will be the result.

The following is a critical test of your organizational leadership skills. Go to the employees who are your direct reports and ask them if your organization (or your division) was successful last year. In addition, ask them what they are using as a measuring stick of success. I did this in my career, and it was a real eye-opener.

I was assigned to a new division within my organization. I was a middle manager. Being newly assigned to this division, I went to my new direct reports individually and asked them, "From your perspective, were we successful as a division last year, and what criteria are you using to measure success?" All of my new direct reports said yes, as a division we were successful last year. But here's the problem, they were all using completely different measures of success. Their measures of success were on opposite ends of the spectrum. Some gave very high-level responses about all of the great work being done in the community and increasing legitimacy in the eyes of the community. Another supervisor said yes because all of his people got to attend the training they wanted to attend. There was no consistency in how they measured success. Every single one of them was rowing in a different direction from their counterparts. Those answers illustrated to me that this division was suffering from a failure of leadership to provide direction. THAT IS A FAILURE OF LEADERSHIP. The reality is each employee was doing what they thought they should be doing and doing it with the best of intentions. But the fact that they all used a different measure of success and, as a result, were all rowing in different directions, meant that it was incumbent upon me to begin providing the much-needed direction.

Here's another test you can do to determine if there is a failure of leadership within your organization. It's similar to the previous question but is also slightly different. Ask your high-level managers to list the top three priorities of your organization. Will they all list the same priorities? I ask this question in my classes, and I get humorous responses. I've had middle managers from the same organization sitting next to each other, and they don't even attempt to list the top three priorities. Instead, they look at each other and begin laughing because before they even try, they already know they won't list the same three priorities. If your high-level managers don't know your top organizational priorities, THAT IS A FAILURE OF LEADERSHIP! This means that the organizational leaders are not providing direction.

I know if this question is asked of the top managers in the vast majority of organizations, the likelihood they will provide the same answers is very, very low. How do I know that?

In 2018, MIT Sloan Management Review published an article titled, *Turning Strategy Into Results.*[4] As part of their research for the article they surveyed more than 10,000 managers across 400 organizations and asked them to list their company's top three to five priorities over the next few years.

In this study the measure of success was set very low. If only two-thirds (66%) of the executives from an organization listed the same priorities, that result was considered a success. This is interesting because in my experience within the academic environment, if you receive a 66% on your test, it's a failing grade. And even though the benchmark for success in this survey was identified at 66%, that

---

4   Donald Sull, Stefano Turconi, Charles Sull, and James Yoder. *MIT Sloan Management Review,* 28 Sept. 2017, sloanreview.mit.edu/article/turning-strategy-into-results/. Accessed 19 Jan. 2020.

score was achieved in only 27% of the companies studied. Conversely, that's a 73% failure rate of companies that couldn't even get to a 66% rate of agreement among their managers. To restate those numbers again, that was 10,000 managers across 400 organizations. What's the likelihood *your* managers are going to list the same top three to five priorities for your organization? If you think that number in your organization is going to be low (and statistically it's very likely it will be low), you have some leadership work to do.

There used to be an instructor who taught classes in the same building where I used to teach. He taught classes to clerical employees. And in every class, he surveyed his students. He'd ask them what their top two frustrations were about the organizations where they worked. After years of conducting this survey he concluded that 80% of all the complaints that students offered in response to his survey could be put into one of two categories:

1. Lack of Direction
2. Micromanagement

Where does micromanagement come from? (I have always considered micromanagement as a red flag identifying an organization that needs my help. I used to tell my friends if they ever overheard someone complaining about micromanagement in the workplace, hand them my business card and ask them to call me to help fix the lack of leadership in their organization.) Micromanagement comes from a boss who has not realized how their leadership role has changed as they got promoted. The role change they are missing is that they should be focusing on results rather than specifically on how a task is done. Great leaders all through history have promoted the idea of focusing on results and letting the ingenuity of your people amaze you as they find creative ways to accomplish the desired results. In General Jim Mattis' book, *Call Sign Chaos*, he talks about a lesson he learned years ago when a company commander trained him in the fine art of artillery fire support. On the final day of training, Mattis was expecting the company commander to control the artillery shots. Instead, the company commander left Mattis alone and watched as Mattis put his new training in artillery fire to work. As Mattis progressed through the live-fire exercise with troops advancing in the field, the company commander nodded and walked away. The message Mattis learned that day was:

Have faith in your subordinates after you have trained them.

That's good advice for all leaders—especially leaders who used to be great technicians. After you have trained your staff, get out of their way and focus on results. If you're not getting the results you want, reexamine the effectiveness of your training instead of going back and grabbing the reigns away from your staff—you're not a technician anymore; you are a coach who focuses on results.

When you have transitioned into the leadership role and are focusing on results, you can now provide the direction your staff so desperately desires, i.e., what are we trying to accomplish, why are we here, and how will we recognize success? This is your leadership job—to provide direction and focus on results.

"Never tell someone how to do something. Just tell them what needs to be done and they will amaze you with their ingenuity."
–General George S. Patton, Jr.

This is an example of a leader who is results-driven and is moving away from micromanagement. Tell your followers what needs to be done (the outcome you expect) and get out of their way.

Former Chairman of the Joint Chiefs of Staff, Martin Dempsey, introduced a concept he called Mission Command in army training and education. The concept of Mission Command is nearly identical to what General Patton stated above. In his book, *Radical Inclusion, What the Post-9/11 World Should Have Taught Us About Leadership*,[5] Dempsey defined Mission Command this way:

Tell your subordinates what you want
accomplished and loosen control to allow them
to develop strategies to achieve the desired outcome.

This is yet another example of a leader focusing on results or outcomes and getting out of the way of their followers. Let them be the technicians you have trained them to be. However, General Jim Mattis made a significant distinction in his book, *Call Sign Chaos*, stating that there is an additional, critical element to add to the results you're describing, and that is to include your intentions.

Mattis said his Marine Corps training taught him to also include the intent, or the "why" of any order he issued. By doing so the intended end-result was always much clearer as the order got relayed to those expected to carry out the order. The method Mattis described was to include within the order the words *"in order to...."* In his book he used this example:

"We will attack that bridge in order to cut off the enemy's escape."

---

5   Dempsey, Martin, and Ori Brafman. *Radical Inclusion: What the Post-9/11 World Should Have Taught Us About Leadership* (Arlington, VA: Missionday, 2018).

If the intent was not included in the order, the troops may attack and hold the bridge, while watching the enemy escape. By including the intent, the troops don't need to call for additional instructions, they already know the intent and can utilize their knowledge, skills, and ability to prevent the enemy from escaping without needing additional instruction.

When employees understand the "why" behind any policy, procedure, or order, it empowers them to make better decisions. When they know "why" a policy exists, i.e., the intent of the policy, the employee is empowered with information that will help them make better decisions. Then, when the employee is confronted with a grey-area decision, they are far more likely to make a good decision that is consistent with the intent of the policy.

I have seen leaders who believe that knowledge is power, and in order to retain their power, they keep information to themselves. They have the insane belief that if the followers know everything the leader knows, the leader is no longer needed. That flawed belief is 100% wrong! If you withhold information, you not only disempower your people, you may potentially be putting them in harm's way. If you believe that by withholding information, you are preserving your importance as a leader, you have two options. Change your belief or resign. Those are your only two options, and I'm very serious about that. Part of your role as a leader is to be a coach and a facilitator of your follower's success—you cannot do that if you are withholding information. If you withhold information, people will not respect you as a leader, and they will not want to work for you. So, for the benefit of your organization, you only have two options.

CHAPTER 18

Employee Engagement

Employee engagement means that workers:

1. Have a strong emotional bond to their organizations,
2. Feel their jobs are important,
3. Are actively involved in and committed to their work,
4. Know their opinions and ideas have value, and
5. Often go beyond their immediate job responsibilities for the good of the organization.

The first three bullet points have a strong tie with the vision and mission statements of the organization, where the vision of the organization appeals to some intrinsic desire within the employee (we will discuss that connection a little later in this book). The fourth bullet connects with a very important little golden nugget of information that I have carried with me for decades, which is something I call the *12-Foot Rule*.

The 12-Foot Rule says that people within 12-feet of a problem should be involved in solving the problem. From a high level, this rule prompts the boss to loosen control and not micromanage, but the benefits go far beyond that. Who knows how better to solve a problem than the people dealing with that problem where it occurs? Perhaps you were a great technician at one time in history, but if you've been in the ivory tower in a management or executive position for any length of time, the environment has changed, and you are likely out-of-touch with the possibilities of the best solution.

This also comes back to the idea of quality control and improving systems. When you get your employees involved in solving a problem, creating that involvement not only increases employee engagement, it also plays a unique role in quality improvement. Making meaningful changes to a system or a process relies on an in-depth understanding of the current system. Only employees involved in the system on a day-to-day basis possess such an understanding. Employing the 12-Foot Rule will not only result in a better solution, but your employees will also be more motivated and engaged because they were able to contribute something valuable in making the process or workplace better.

In his book, *Quality Performance Excellence—Management, Organization, and Strategy*, James R. Evans describes a 12-Foot Rule success at Southwest Airlines. Evans' book describes the event like this:[6]

In 2002 fuel costs had tripled and Southwest Airlines was in financial trouble as a result. The former CEO Herb Kelleher decided to implement the 12-Foot Rule by sending a letter to the home of every Southwest Airlines employee describing the financial threat the company was up against and asked for ideas from each employee on ways to cut costs. In his letter he said if every employee could figure out a way to save just $5.00 per day, the crisis could be averted.

Within days employees responded with all sorts of cost-saving ideas. A group of mechanics suggested ways to reduce costs of heating aircraft, another unit offered to do its own janitorial work. Within two weeks the suggestions offered by employees totaled a $2 million savings.

Do you think CEO Kelleher could have generated these savings from the ivory tower? No. He was smart enough to employ the 12-Foot Rule and engage the experts where the "rubber meets the road."

---

6   Evans, James R. *Quality & Performance Excellence: Management, Organization and Strategy*, 5th ed. (Mason, OH: Thomson Business and Economics, 2008).

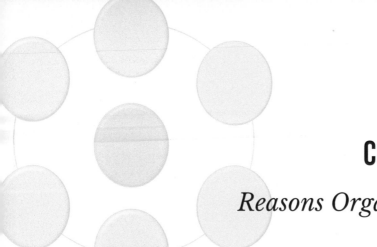

CHAPTER 19

Reasons Organizations Flounder

Because of my long career in law enforcement, when I post the following list in class, the PowerPoint slide has a title that says, Reasons Police Agencies Flounder. But this list applies to all organizations, both non-profit and for-profit organizations.

Why Organizations Flounder

1. No Leadership or Bad Leadership (Technicians at the Executive Level)
2. No Shared Vision (Mission and Values)
3. No Goals and Strategic Plan
4. Failure to Understand "Systems"
5. No Accountability to Defined Standards
6. Lack of Employee Empowerment

To illustrate this point, I use a real-life example of which I have become aware. My intention is not to embarrass anyone or any organization. My intent is to debrief what occurred as a learning experience so that we can all learn from these events and utilize these experiences to create a better future for our organizations moving forward.

To maintain anonymity, we will call the police department in this example, Anytown Police Department (and from my experience, this really could be any town and any police department).

In 2009, outside consultants were hired to conduct an employee survey and a systems analysis of the Anytown Police Department. The reason the outside consultants were hired was because there was a lot of turmoil within the department and a huge chasm existed between management and labor. The internal problems were so significant that the consultant's final report referred to these problems as having "…necessitated this form of 'intervention.'" The consultant's final 21-page report depicted an organization in turmoil and listed many deficiencies that were related to the leadership of the department. The list of deficiencies included, but was not limited to:

- Lack of a clear vision, mission, and values statement
- Lack of officer empowerment
- Issues with poor communication
- Micromanagement through burdensome policies, procedures, and directives

The following is a brief synopsis of the descriptors provided in the consultant's report.

Lack of a clear vision, mission, and values statement

Without purpose, leading becomes motion without meaning… activity without vision…and results without significance. The following articulates a couple of reasons police agencies are likely to experience difficulty in managing their operations.

1. No shared vision (mission and values)
2. No strategic plan and goals

There appears to be no viable strategic plan that clearly outlines the vision or values of the department. It is ultimately the responsibility of upper management to establish a viable mission and vision, in collaboration with stakeholders, customers, and staff. That does not appear to have been done at [APD] and has resulted in a variety of organizational challenges. Consequently, in the absence of direction, individuals and/or groups within the organization develop their own sense of purpose and direction.

Lack of officer empowerment

Line officers need to feel empowered to make decisions. The bottom line is the [Anytown] Police Officers report they do not feel empowered. Empowerment embodies the belief that decision making should be the province of individuals, not policies or procedures. This perceived sense of disempowerment has led to a very serious morale problem in the rank and file of the [Anytown] Police Department.

Issues with poor communication

Meaningful communication up and down the chain of command in the [Anytown] Police Department appears to be essentially non-existent. Employees at every level are sensitive to formal communications that may appear to have a "hidden" agenda. This is symptomatic of the "trust" issues evident at [APD].

Micromanagement through burdensome policies, procedures, and directives

In many instances the implementation of policies and procedures were the result of individuals making poor decisions. Rather than address the individual, a policy statement or directive would subsequently be formulated and distributed to avoid recurrence of the problem situation. This strategy suggests that everyone has violated the particular rule and ultimately promotes an atmosphere of fear and mistrust. The officers feel encumbered with a multitude of policies or directives and constrained to make decisions. In the final analysis, policies and procedures in most organizations are designed to "constrain" behavior. Avoiding failure is not a formula for success.

Ultimately, values transcend situation… policies don't. From a leadership perspective, it would seem you would want officers to make decisions based on values, not on what they can remember to do…or not do.

This gives you a brief snapshot of what the consultant's report contained. Ultimately, the contents of the consultant's report led to the police chief's resignation. For the purposes of this book, we are going to focus on one of the issues identified in the report: a lack of clear vision and mission statements and a lack of a strategic plan.

In January of 2011, the City of Anytown hired a new police chief. You would think the new police chief could use the consultant's 21-page report as a roadmap to organizational success. Well, if you thought that might be the case, you'd be wrong. The new chief tossed out the consultant's report. For the next eight years, all the way through 2019, nothing changed within the Anytown Police Department regarding the lack of clear vision, mission, and values statements. The department's vision, mission, and values statements remained unchanged, and neither the vision statement nor mission statement were used as a guiding principle for the operational procedures of the department.

By 2015, the command staff was growing weary waiting for guidance from their new leader, so they created and submitted to the chief a four-page document outlining six steps for strategic planning.

1. Define the organization's mission and vision
2. Assess the current strengths and weaknesses of the organization
3. Set objectives for the organization
4. Create strategies to achieve the objectives
5. Implement the strategies
6. Monitor progress and adapt the strategic plan as necessary

On August 18, 2015, in response to this four-page document, the chief, deputy chief, and eight command staff personnel attended an all-day off-site retreat to focus specifically on strategic planning. However, at the retreat, the chief refused to take any action on Step 1 (defining the organization's vision and mission) and instead, moved directly to Step 2, a SWOT analysis (Strengths, Weaknesses, Opportunities, and Threats).

In the strategic planning process, the steps are in a specific order for a reason—each step is a foundational step for the next step, and if you don't do one step, it is impossible to move to the next step. Step 1 is to define vision and mission statements. A vision statement is an aspirational statement of what you would like the organization to achieve. It's a forward-looking statement of where the organization is going. A mission statement is a public declaration of why the organization exists. (We'll cover these definitions in more detail shortly.) If you don't do Step 1, defining where the organization is going, how can you build a plan to get there?

In this case, on August 18, 2015, at the chief's direction, the group moved to Step 2, a SWOT analysis where the strengths and weaknesses of the organization were analyzed. The SWOT analysis predictably revealed that the major weakness of the police department was a lack of focus on key objectives. The organization had no direction from the leader, and, as a result, it had no plan for how to get anywhere, so it's no wonder the organization had no key objectives because it had no plan. In the meeting, the command staff used descriptive phrases like "the shiny object syndrome" and "the squirrel syndrome" to describe the weaknesses of the organization and to describe how there seemed to be a new top objective at each week's command staff meeting. It seemed there was always a new top priority based on whatever meeting(s) the chief had attended the previous week. The organization had no focus. Every week it was something different.

The off-site retreat lasted all day and never got any further than Step 2. Subsequently, and throughout all of 2019, nothing changed regarding the leadership of the organization. In October of 2019, the police chief retired, and a new chief was appointed from within the department. This new chief had not been part of the command staff during the 2015 retreat because, at that time, he was a first-level supervisor. At the time of this writing, the new chief has not taken any steps to create new vision or mission statements and has taken no steps to develop a strategic plan or define any key objectives. And why would he? That type of leadership behavior has never been mentored within this organization. It's a classic case of not knowing what you don't know.

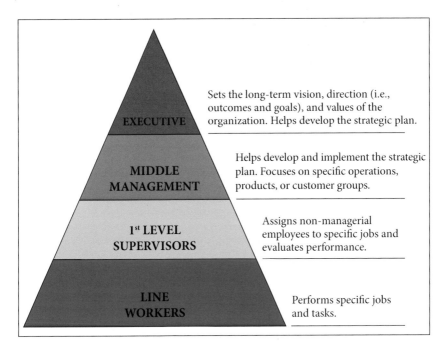

Figure 19.1 An Organizational Pyramid

The organizational pyramid shown in Figure 19.1 depicts the different responsibilities of each level as you move up through the organization. For most organizations, there is little or no mentoring in regard to the differences between functioning as a first-level supervisor and functioning as an executive.

Many executives conduct themselves as first-level supervisors—because that is all they know—which leads to a lack of direction and results in micromanagement within the organization—and ultimately, organizational failure. Leadership at the first-level supervisor level occurs in a face-to-face environment and does not include creating direction for the organization. In executive-level leadership, influence and inspiration from the leader may come in a situation where there is never face-to-face contact, and the executive-level leader is responsible for sense-making, and direction-setting for the organization. How do you lead (influence and inspire) without face-to-face interaction? It's an entirely different skill set. And yet many, if not most, executive-level leaders do not understand this difference because it was never mentored within their organization, or they were never exposed to this concept by reading leadership books or within an academic environment.

All organizations need smart leaders. It's not enough to merely be "…a really nice person" or charismatic. The police chief mentioned earlier was a really nice guy; everyone liked him. But being a nice guy did not make him an effective executive-level leader. We need smart executives who know how to be executives. The entire management team needs to understand this conceptual part of organizational leadership in order to be successful. This book alone is not enough. Effective leaders need to be life-long learners.

When I teach my classes there is one thing that truly frustrates me, which is when I have police chiefs that are in my class (because my class is required by the State Training Commission) and the chiefs sit in class with a closed posture and their inflated egos create an attitude of, "You can't teach me anything; I already know everything I need to know." As a leader, the day you think you know everything is the day you are done. An important point to remember is attributed to Bill Nye, the Science Guy. Bill is attributed with saying, "Everyone you meet knows something that you don't know." Which is an excellent segue into the next chapter about smart leadership and management.

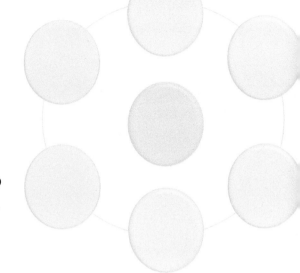

CHAPTER 20

Smart Leadership and Management

It all starts at the top with Vision, Mission, and Goals. If you are the leader of an organization or a workgroup, you should ask yourself:

- Do I have a plan?
- What is my vision of what this organization or division should become or achieve?

Vision is a potent force within organizations that can initiate fantastic energy and momentum.

Energy and momentum come from having a clear vision of what the organization strives to achieve. It thrives with a well-thought-out plan to attain that vision, which is carefully conceived and communicated in a way that lets everybody take an interest in and ownership of accomplishing these plans. This energy and momentum are valuable and essential to a healthy organization. It is the feeling among a cohort of individuals that they are entwined as a team and moving toward a recognizable and meaningful objective.

The purpose of the vision is not only to achieve a meaningful strategic or company goal but also to attract like-minded people to your organization as well as inspire those who are already within your organization. A meaningful vision defines where the organization is going. When someone's heart and soul connect with the intent of that vision; connects with the belief of the vision, they will commit to the aspirations of the organization, and they will commit with their blood, sweat, and tears. Therefore, the most important function of a leader is to develop a clear and compelling picture of the future and to secure commitment to that ideal. Former CEO of Johnson and Johnson, James Burke, estimated he spent 40 percent of his time communicating and reinforcing the company's vision.

Visions can be small or large and can exist at any organizational level. However, when they exist at the division-level, they must be in alignment with and support the organization's overall vision. Many leaders fail because they do not have a vision—instead, they focus on surviving on a day-by-day basis. This is what I call *organizational drift*. When the leader becomes so consumed with the daily demands of the workplace that they lose connection with their purpose as a leader, the organization begins to drift because it has no direction from its leader. Whatever the hot issue is of the day, that hot issue becomes the new top priority.

In his book, *Call Sign Chaos*, General Mattis describes how he struggled with this issue.

He said it's easy for observers to suggest telling your support staff to be more efficient. However, there are often things that can only be addressed by the executive in-charge. In Mattis's case, issues that needed his immediate attention were incidents of commercial ships being attacked by pirates. Or perhaps a foreign leader had an urgent question, or the Secretary of Defense needed some information before departing on an international trip. Or perhaps it was an ambassador requesting military assistance related to refugee support, or a Special Operations commander needing to convey information about a terrorist sighting in a sensitive area.

While these examples are all related to Mattis' experience as a military executive, executives in all organizations can relate to the constant stream of urgent matters that come across their desks every day.

Mattis talks about how these daily urgent matters consumed so much of his time that he struggled to find time to reflect on the critical issues that were essential for senior decision-makers to contemplate. As the executive, he needed to question the tactics they were using. Was there anything that needed to be done that wasn't getting done? Were there any weaknesses or gaps in their strategy? What might the enemy's response be tomorrow or next week? Mattis struggled as he knew all of these considerations required more time in a day than he was able to reserve for those purposes. But he knew he couldn't fall into organizational drift; he had to reserve time in his day for these critical executive-level considerations.

No one said leadership at the executive level is easy. Like in Mattis' case, there are constant demands on your time. However, a leader must be disciplined enough to recognize when they are drifting away from their primary purpose of providing direction to the organization, which takes us into the importance of creating a vision statement and a strategic plan.

CHAPTER 21

Creating a Vision Statement and Building a Plan

As mentioned earlier, a vision statement is an aspirational statement of what the organization aspires to achieve or aspires to become. It is a forward-looking statement that looks toward the future of the organization. A vision statement is like an architectural rendering that is drawn with words.

As the organizational leader you need to create a vision in your mind's eye of what the future of the organization is going to look like, or what it's going to accomplish. Once you have that vision, you now need to translate that image into words (the *vision statement*) so when other people read those words, it creates the same image in their mind's eye as you saw in yours. This is a very conceptual idea and the best way I have found to make the concept more relatable is to use the example of building your dream home. That's why I use the phrase "your vision statement is like an architectural rendering that is drawn with words."

The time has come in your life to build the home of your dreams. You hire an architect and you describe to them what you see in your mind's eye. It includes the approximate square footage, a bedroom and bathroom count, living spaces and the functionality of each, and the number of parking spaces in the garage. The architect begins putting your ideas to paper and eventually creates an architectural rendering of your dream home (Figure 21.1).

Figure 21.1 Your Dream Home—an Architectural Rendering

This architectural rendering represents what we aspire to create for our dream home. The architect created this picture so that everyone can view the same image, and everyone gets a good understanding of what you're trying to build. The challenge with a vision statement is that it is an architectural rendering drawn with words rather than with images. But the hope is when others read your vision statement, the "picture" it creates in their mind helps them get a good understanding of what you're trying to build.

Now that the vision of our dream home is complete, it's time to create a plan for how to make the vision a reality. In business, we call this a *strategic plan*. In home building, it's called a construction plan, but the processes are nearly identical. Your architect will create blueprints and a construction plan. The construction plan will contain major objectives that need to be completed in a specific order because some objectives are built on the foundation of previous objectives. For example, the first objective will be to get the blueprints reviewed by the local building authority and obtain construction permits. The subsequent major objectives may be the dirt work, framing, roofing and siding, etc.

Each major objective will contain subordinate tasks that, when combined, result in the completion of the major objective. For example, the major objective of completing the dirt work may include site excavation, digging for the foundation, pouring the footings, and installing the underground utilities, including natural gas, water, and electricity. After these tasks are complete, the next tasks could be pouring the foundation, grading for the driveway, and landscaping.

The next major objective may be the framing, which may include erecting the exterior walls, the interior walls, the roof framing, and the subflooring. Of course, the dirt work objective has to be completed before the framing objective can begin.

The next major objective (after framing) may be roofing and siding, which will include the subordinate steps of roof sheathing and shingles, wall sheathing and wrap, windows and doors, and siding. Of course, the dirt work and framing objectives must be completed before we can begin work on the roofing and siding objective. It may be helpful to create a Gantt chart to map out the interdependencies of each objective and sub-step contained in the project.

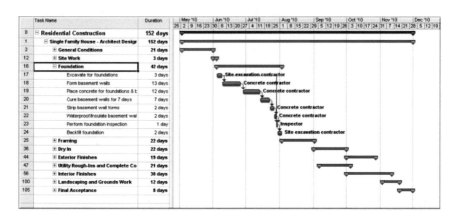

Figure 21.2 A Gantt Chart of the Project Plan

Figure 21.2 is a sample Gantt chart. In this Gantt chart you can see the major objectives of the project, which include the general conditions, site work, foundation, framing, dry in, exterior finishes, etc. In addition, each major objective can be expanded to show all of the tasks that must be finished before that part of the project is complete.

Now that we have our construction plan, all of the steps are mapped out on the calendar and we are ready to begin the project of making the vision of our dream home a reality. As we go through the construction process, do you think there might be some delays? Of course, there will be. Inclement weather, possible flooding, contractors who don't show up on time (or who don't show up at all), building materials that are back-ordered, the building inspector refuses to sign-off on some part of the work, etc.

Do you think there may be change orders along the way as well? Of course, there will be. Even with the best-prepared plans in place, you will discover flaws in the planning process. Perhaps a door swing blocks access to a cabinet or blocks access to another door, resulting in a change-order. Or as the walls are erected, you begin to get a feel for how the space is going to be and you decide you want the kitchen laid out differently, which results in a change-order. All of these things are going to happen during the construction process. And they will also occur during the execution of your strategic plan for your business. Just like in your construction plan, when these interrupting events do occur, you will make adjustments based upon the type of interruption, coupled with the new information you have just learned, and keep moving forward until your vision becomes a reality. When the vision becomes a reality, you can sit back and enjoy your accomplishment. Remember, it all started with a vision!

CHAPTER 22

Vision Statements Appeal to Intrinsic Motivation

"One of the most powerful internal motivators on the planet is a sense of meaning and purpose."

Kouzes, James M. and Barry Z. Posner. *The Truth About Leadership: The No-Fads, Heart-of-the-Matter Facts You Need to Know* (Plano, TX: Jossey-Bass, 2010).

Having a sense of meaning and purpose is the sort of internal motivator that results when an employee both connects with and identifies with your vision statement. It's the resultant motivation when the employee says to themselves, "I want to be part of that." This sort of connection exists when the purpose of the organization and what the organization aspires to accomplish connect with the employee's heart and soul, i.e., the employee's natural calling in life. The amount they are paid is secondary to being part of something meaningful; something that is larger than themselves.

On the Internet, you can find different versions of a fictional story about two stonemasons, which illustrates this concept. The story says you are traveling through the European countryside hundreds of years ago when you come across two stonemasons who are hard at work in the hot summer sun chiseling large boulders to build some sort of structure. You walk up to the first stonemason and ask him, "Do you like your job?"

The man replies, "You know, I've been building this wall for as long as I can remember. The work's monotonous; I work in the scorching hot sun all day long. The stones are heavy and lifting them day after day can be backbreaking. And I'm not even sure if this project will be completed in my lifetime. But hey... it's a job... and it pays the bills."

You thank the man for his time, and you continue on your walk. About 100 feet away, you come across a second stonemason and ask him the same question, "Do you like your job?"

The second stonemason looks up at you. You can see the sunlight glisten in the sweat as it drips off his brow. He puts down his hammer and chisel, and then stands to look you in the eye. Before he says anything, he pulls a small rag from his back pocket and wipes the sweat from his forehead. He then replies in a voice filled with great enthusiasm and commitment, "I love my job! I'm building a cathedral. You know, I've been building this wall for as long as I can remember. The work's monotonous; I work in the scorching hot sun all day long. The stones are heavy and lifting them day after day can be backbreaking. And I'm not even sure if this project will be completed in my lifetime."

"But... I'm building a cathedral that will be used as a place of worship for hundreds, if not thousands, of years. A place that will be used by many as a place of sanctuary and solace. I love my work; it's my contribution to what I'm helping to create. My work here is my small contribution to something that will be great."

Here we have two men doing the same job. One man is inspired only by the paycheck that pays his bills. The other finds inspiration in the vision of what he's building. In all likelihood, where do you think this vision came from? You can be rest assured that the vision came from the faith leader, perhaps from the Bishop. It came from the leader who had a vision of the future; a vision of what was needed and the ability to communicate the importance of that vision to others. This story is an example of what a powerful motivator a good vision statement can be.

Here's a little golden nugget you can keep in the back of your mind to help illustrate this point. Working hard at something you don't care about is called stress. Working hard at something you do care about is called passion. Now let's look at an example that is the antithesis of passion where there is no connection between the work and a larger purpose.

This story, the story of King Sisyphus, comes from Greek mythology. King Sisyphus was a cruel king. He was so cruel to his people that the Greek Gods decided that Sisyphus needed to be punished for the cruelty he bestowed upon his people.

As punishment, the Greek Gods forced Sisyphus to roll an immense boulder up to the top of a hill. It would take Sisyphus all day to push this boulder to the top of the hill, and it would take every ounce of energy he had. For Sisyphus, it was an entire day of grunting, groaning, and straining. It was a Herculean effort to get this immense boulder to the top of the hill.  At the end of the day, when Sisyphus finally got the boulder to the top of the hill, the boulder would roll back down, all the way to the bottom. Sisyphus' punishment was to repeat this task every day, for eternity. This was a task that had no purpose; a task that had no meaning. This was a task where a person would rather die than be subjected to this punishment.

Are there employees in your organization doing work they feel has no purpose? Are there employees in your organization who, absent the paycheck, would rather be dead than be subjected to the meaningless work they do? Is it possible the work they do actually does have meaning and does contribute to a larger, meaningful purpose, but they have merely lost sight of that connection? Is it possible they have lost sight of that connection because management and leadership within the organization fail to help them see the importance of their work? Let's move on to an example of work where the connection to a meaningful purpose could easily be lost if management and leadership allowed it to become lost.

This story occurred in 1962 when President John F. Kennedy was visiting the NASA Space Center in Florida. President Kennedy walked up to one man and asked him, "What do you do here?" The man, with his chest held high, replied proudly to the President by saying, "I'm helping put a man on the moon." The job title of that man who gave such a proud reply was the janitor. This proud man understood his role in the organizational machine called NASA, and he knew that if he didn't do his job of maintaining the facility properly, it could adversely impact the efficiency and effectiveness of the effort to put a man on the moon. He knew that although his function was different, as part of the NASA machine, he knew his job was just as important as the person who would push the launch button, or the men who would sit at the pointy end of the rocket.

A business organization is similar to the mechanical mechanism inside of a clock. Inside of a clock, there are a lot of different springs, wheels, and cogs, all doing distinctly different roles yet all working in harmony to accomplish  the mission—which is to display the time of day. And while there are so many moving parts, no single part is any more, or any less, important than any other. If any of the springs, wheels, or cogs fails to do its job, the whole machine will come to a grinding halt. And your organization operates in the same way.

While your organization may not come to a grinding halt if one person fails to do their job, your organization will not run as effectively or efficiently as it should. That's why it's so important to have a compelling vision statement and hire people who believe in that vision.

> "If you hire people just because they can do a job they will work for your money. But if you hire people because they believe what you believe—they will work for you with blood, sweat, and tears."

> –Simon Sinek, 2009 TEDx Talk,
> How Great Leaders Inspire Action

The above quote was taken from Simon Sinek's 2009 TEDx Puget Sound talk. This talk is available on YouTube and may be one of the most viewed videos of all of the TED Talks. I show this video in my classes, and I highly encourage you to search YouTube for the video and watch it. The video focuses on understanding the "why" of what you do. It illustrates the concept that when people believe in your "why," they will demonstrate an amazing commitment to your purpose or your cause.

The National Geographic television channel used to have a show called *Chain of Command*. In this show, which was produced in 2016 and 2017, National Geographic was given unprecedented access to the stories of the men and women of the US Armed Forces fighting the global war on violent extremism.

In one of the episodes, there were numerous examples of high-level military leaders making sure the troops understood "why" they were in Iraq. At the beginning of the episode, you hear this quote, "At the end of the day, what military service is about is being a part of something greater than yourself." That is precisely the point we have been making in this book, which is the importance of a meaningful vision statement and how it relates to intrinsic motivation—being part of something greater than yourself.

Other quotes in the episode that illustrate how important it is for a leader to convey to their people the understanding of "why" they are doing what they're doing include:

- "...[these meetings] are also a chance to make sure everyone down the chain of command knows why they're here."
- "I want to give you a sense of what you're doing here—the larger mission that you're a part of. It's really important."
- "Lt. General Townsend provides clarity of purpose to the men and women savings lives on the battlefield."

This episode of *Chain of Command* is a perfect illustration of high-level military leaders getting out into the field and speaking face-to-face with their troops to make sure the soldiers understand the "why" of their mission, and the "why" they are in Iraq. Those military leaders realize how important that understanding is to intrinsic motivation. And while conveying that message is very important, remember, as a leader, you have to communicate that message frequently. As stated earlier in this book, the former CEO of Johnson and Johnson, James Burke, estimated he spent 40% of his time conveying this type of information.

Another important "why" factor that you need to understand in business is why do we exist as an organization, which takes us right into the next chapter where we will discuss Mission Statements.

CHAPTER 23

Mission Statements

A mission statement is a public declaration of "why" your organization exists. It's that simple. It is a completely descriptive statement of who you are as an organization, what your organization does, and why your organization exists.

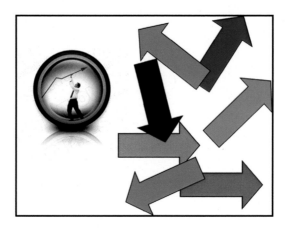

Without strong vision and mission statements, the work efforts of employees in any enterprise will be disorganized, dysfunctional, and completely inefficient—leading to employee frustration and a substandard work product—or no work product at all.

In the absence of direction, people will fill the void and create their own direction. They'll most likely do it with the best of intentions, i.e., they'll start doing what they *think* they should be doing. But if your staff isn't in alignment because they're not getting direction from leadership, at best they're in competition with each other.

Employees at all levels of the organization from the executive suite at the top, all the way down to the line-level have three "needs to know," which are:

1. They need to know the grand plan—the purpose, values, and strategies for success for the organization;
2. They need to know what is expected of them personally, and why;
3. They need to have feedback on individual performance, with recognition for their efforts.

I used to use an exercise in my classes that caused the students to physically experience the personal emotions felt when working under a lack of direction. The scenario caused so much frustration for the students that I stopped making them work through the exercise, and instead, I discussed what previous students had experienced. The old exercise was called, "Where the Money Ends."

In this exercise, I would collect one dollar from each student. (They'd be given advance notice to bring a one-dollar bill.) I would then pick two students who I would appoint as directors and have them move to the back of the classroom. I gave the money I collected to the directors. I would then divide the remaining students into four groups and have each group appoint one person from their group as a middle manager. Everyone else would be considered line employees.

I would display these instructions on the screen, and they would be the only instructions the students would receive for this exercise.

- The mission of the organization is to develop proposals that deal with the following: "Ways to improve the quality of work life for personnel in an organization."

- The line staff will prepare proposals and make presentations on "Ways to improve the quality of work life for personnel in an organization."
- The middle managers handle all communication between line employees and the directors.
- The directors decide which proposals will be accepted or denied, and also determine how much funding to give each proposal. Also, the directors cannot directly communicate with the line employees; they must communicate through the middle managers.
- The exercise will last for one hour, and where the money is at the end of the hour is where it will stay. Begin!

Within a short period of time, all of the students would become frustrated by the lack of direction and guidance in the exercise. The directors were not sure what they were trying to accomplish, or how their role was defined toward accomplishing the mission. The middle managers and line employees also shared the same frustration— they didn't understand what they were trying to accomplish, and they didn't know how their role fit into the big picture. As a group, they struggled and they floundered. Then, and here's the critical part...they began to fill in the void of information with their own speculation on what they were trying to accomplish.

The purpose of the money exercise was for the students to experience first-hand what it's like to be part of an organization that provides inadequate guidance to its employees. The students personally experienced that with inadequate direction or guidance, the resulting work effort is:

- Disorganized
- Dysfunctional
- Completely inefficient
- Leads to employee frustration
- Results in a substandard work product, or no product at all
- Employees will fill the void of information with their own speculation

The money exercise is an excellent first-hand experience that helps to drive home the importance of good vision and mission statements. However, providing guidance and direction does not stop with the creation of the vision and mission statements.

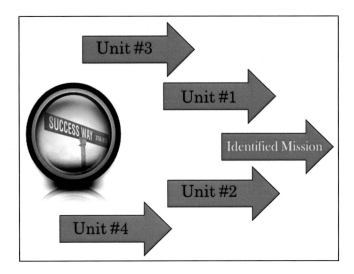

Management needs to make sure all of the work units within the organization are aligned and consistent with the mission. Like the internal workings of a clock, not everyone is performing the same task; they obviously will be performing different functions. However, management needs to make sure all of the individual functions are aligned toward mission accomplishment.

CHAPTER 24

Examples of Vision and Mission Statements

My favorite example of good vision and mission statements comes from Charity Water, a non-profit organization. The reason this is my favorite is because of its simplicity, and yet it still provides perfect descriptors. This is an ideal example of how vision and mission statements don't need to be lengthy and wordy. As a matter of fact, the more succinct you can make your statements, the better they'll be remembered and understood.

Remember, a mission statement is: A public declaration of why your organization exists. Charity Water's mission statement is: *We're a non-profit organization bringing clean, safe, drinking water to people in developing countries.*

A mission statement doesn't get much more concise than that. And as you can read, that statement describes perfectly why Charity Water exists as an organization. Now let's look at their vision statement.

Remember, a vision statement is an aspirational statement of what you aspire to achieve or aspire to become as an organization. Charity Water's vision statement: *We believe we can end the water crisis in our lifetime by ensuring that every person on the planet has access to life's most basic need—clean drinking water.*

Wow! A clear and concise statement of what they aspire to achieve. But more importantly, imagine if you're the type of person who has a great desire to help developing countries. Maybe you're the type of person who has volunteered on a mission in developing countries to build housing. Or perhaps you've donated your medical expertise, or other forms of expertise, to help people who are struggling in developing countries. In this case, the vision statement of Charity Water may speak to your heart and soul. And if it does, how hard would you work for Charity Water? Would you be inspired by the paycheck, or would you be inspired to be part of something meaningful and be inspired by helping to save lives around the world? This is an example of how a clear, vivid, and meaningful vision statement can stimulate intrinsic motivation in your workplace.

Let's look at the mission statement of the American Heart Association: *To be a relentless force for a world of longer, healthier lives.*

Again, that's a pretty concise statement of why the AHA exists as an organization. I couldn't find a vision statement for the American Heart Association, but I did find their 2020 goal, which certainly sounds like a vision statement to me: *The American Heart Association is working to improve cardiovascular health of all Americans by 20 percent, and reduce deaths from cardiovascular diseases and stroke by 20 percent, by the year 2020.*

While this statement is longer in word count, it's still pretty clear what they aspire to achieve by the year 2020.

Before we move on to strategic planning, I want to leave you with a final thought about effective vision statements.

Leadership is dreaming of a dream and then making it come true. Leaders create clear and worthy images that motivate the organization and then create a climate so that ideas are transformed into deeds.

–George Manning. *The Art of Leadership*, 5th ed. (New York, NY: McGraw-Hill Higher Education, 2014).

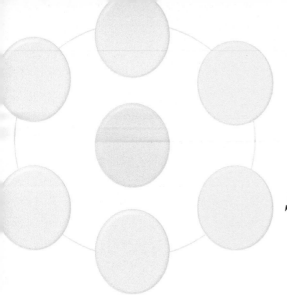

CHAPTER 25

Strategic Planning

Strategic plans set primary objectives and strategies for how to allocate resources (human and capital) to make your vision statement a reality.

Organizations that execute well (the ability to deliver on their most strategic goals and priorities) do four things very consistently:

1. People actually know the goals of the organization.
2. They know what to do to achieve their goals.
3. They know how they are doing against the measures of the goals.
4. There is clear accountability for results.

Item number one above takes us back to the 2017 Top Priorities Survey where 10,000+ managers across 400 organizations were asked to list the top priorities of their organization. Remember how only two-thirds of managers listed the same priorities in only 27% of the companies surveyed? We have to do a better job of communicating what our organizational goals are. That is a crucial role of top management: to provide direction.

Figure 25.1 is an illustration of the theory of Servant Leadership. Even though this pyramid is inverted, it shows how in the theory of Servant Leadership, the role of leaders and managers is to support frontline workers. And notice the role of the top executives hasn't changed. As seen in this inverted pyramid, the role of top executives is still to keep the mission and strategies clear. That's just another way of saying, provide direction.

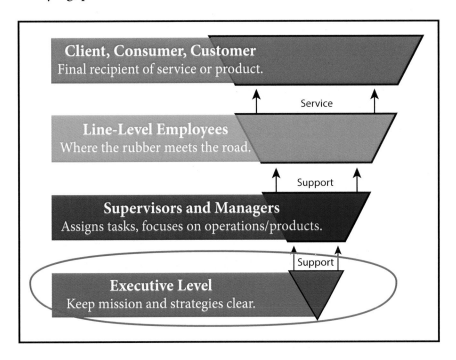

Figure 25.1 Servant Leadership Model

Remember when we talked about how the architect creates a construction plan for your dream home in Chapter 21? Now it's time to build the construction plan to make your vision statement become a reality. In business, we call this a strategic plan.

Initially, you should start thinking from a high-level view of what steps are necessary to make your vision a reality. If you've never done a strategic plan, DO NOT make it overly complicated. Doing *some* planning is better than no planning at all. Strategic plans can get very detailed and complex, but they don't have to be. As you become more experienced with doing strategic planning, you will get better, and you'll probably learn new analytical tools along the way. Some of those tools include:

- The Fit Test—How well does the strategy fit the organization's situation?
- The Competitive Advantage Test—does the strategy achieve sustainable competitive advantage?
- The Performance Test—is the strategy producing good company performance?
- Resource and Capability Analysis—identify the most robust resources to achieve the bottom-line results.

The details of these analytical tools are beyond the scope of this book, but I want you to be aware that additional tools are available when you're ready to utilize them.

During strategic planning, leaders formulate a path to success that guides how people set priorities, allocate resources, and plan how to achieve key goals.

Strategic planning includes six basic steps:

1. Define the organization's vision and mission.
   a. Identify what you aspire to achieve or aspire to accomplish as an organization, and also describe why you exist as an organization.
2. SWOT Analysis
   a. Strengths, Weaknesses, Opportunities, Threats
3. Setting organizational objectives
4. Tactical planning
   a. Setting strategies to accomplish objectives
5. Implementing the strategy
   a. Middle managers or supervisors actually implement a strategy.

6. Evaluating results
   a. Did you hit the target? If not, adjust the inputs or objectives to achieve success.

1. Define the Organization's Vision and Mission

We've already described the purpose of a strong vision statement and mission statement, but I'll add one more point we didn't discuss previously. When you go through this strategic planning process, it is vital to communicate the new vision and mission statements throughout the entire organization. And hopefully, in creating the new vision and mission, you involved several employees from all levels of the organization, and perhaps even a few external stakeholders as well.

If you watched Simon Sinek's 2009 TEDx Puget Sound talk video that was mentioned in Chapter 22, you heard Simon talk about the Law of Diffusion of Innovation, and he spoke of the "tipping point." He mentions how you can't achieve mass-market appeal until you get past the tipping point. That includes the innovators at the front of the curve; they are the ones who just "get it." But more importantly, these are the people in your organization who believe in your cause— because they just get it. Then you also have your early adopters before you get to the tipping point. The innovators are your informal leaders in your organization, and you'll likely find many informal as well as formal leaders in the early adopter category as well. If you want to succeed in having the organization adopt your new vision, you must get these people involved early in the process. They are your internal salespeople who will do the most to convince the late adopters and laggards to get on board with the new mission. If you want success in this organizational change, you must bring those people who are ahead of the tipping point into the process early and get them involved in creating the new future of the organization. Once you cross that "tipping point," you are far more likely to get mass organizational appeal for the new vision of the future.

2. SWOT Analysis

SWOT analysis stands for Strengths, Weaknesses, Opportunities, and Threats. Strengths and Weaknesses are generally internal characteristics of your organization, and Opportunities and Threats are usually external factors influencing your organization. This step allows you to assess your internal and external environments before moving on to Step 3, setting organizational objectives.

3. Setting Organizational Objectives

As organizational leaders, you must agree on the organization's current condition/status (facilitated by Step 2 above), agree on where you want to take the organization, and establish a plan to get there. While the vision and mission statements identify the organization's overall goals and direction, objectives are more concrete. Initially, new objectives should focus on internal processes that have the most significant impact on the services you are currently providing (i.e., the weaknesses identified in Step 2). Once current objectives, programs, and processes are deemed to be performing at optimal levels, then additional objectives can be added, or you can decide to replace outdated or obsolete activities.

The relationship between goals, objectives, and strategies can be somewhat confusing, but don't let that relationship get in the way of working through your planning process. The relationship between goals, objectives, and strategies is not chiseled in stone, and you can do whatever makes sense for your organization. Remember, it is always better to do some planning rather than no planning at all. If this categorization of goals and objectives is burdensome, do what makes sense to you. However, with that being said, most companies keep their strategic plans private, so for an example of a strategic plan, we must turn to the public sector.

The Tucson, Arizona police department has its strategic plan on its website, and the strategic plan serves as an excellent example of the hierarchical relationship among goals, objectives, and strategies. Their 2013–2018 strategic plan had six major goals:[7]

- Goal 1: Reduce, prevent, and solve crime
- Goal 2: Improve quality of life issues
- Goal 3: Embrace and integrate technology throughout the agency
- Goal 4: Strengthen communication
- Goal 5: Achieve organizational excellence to provide superior service
- Goal 6: Develop and retain a quality workforce

Goal 1 has three subordinate objectives listed as 1.1, 1.2, and 1.3. The first subordinate objective is listed as 1.1 Establish Effective Enforcement Initiatives. Objective 1.1 then has ten subordinate strategies listed as 1.1.1, 1.1.2, 1.1.3, 1.1.4, etc.

Subordinate objective 1.2 Enhance Investigative Initiatives has 15 subordinate strategies.

The strategic plan of the Tucson police department is a very clear illustration of the hierarchical relationship among goals, objectives, and strategies and may stimulate some ideas for building the strategic plan for your organization.

4. Tactical Planning

These are all of the sub-steps underlying a major objective that must be cumulatively accomplished in order to achieve the overall objective; this is where the rubber meets the road—this is where the work gets done. Tactical planning will include the logistics and management of both capital and human resources.

---

7   Tucson Police Department. *Tucson Police Department Strategic Plan 2013–2018*, https://www.tucsonaz.gov/files/police/SPFinal.pdf. Accessed 19 Jan. 2020.

Included in the logistical plan is the identification of Key Performance Indicators (KPIs) or success measurements, i.e., how will you know when you have succeeded, or whether you are on the path to success?

Today we operate in such complex environments you will likely have more than one key performance indicator. Just like the idea that a pilot would not focus on only one instrument in the cockpit. A pilot cannot focus solely on airspeed, ignoring the altimeter or fuel gauge, and likewise cannot focus exclusively on the altimeter, ignoring airspeed and fuel levels. In the cockpit, there are a variety of key performance indicators that need to be monitored in order to keep the plane airborne. Likewise, your work environment will likely have multiple key performance indicators in order to make sure you remain in business.

5. Implementing the Strategy

Now that you have your strategic plan constructed, it is time to implement the plan. However, now you must continually monitor the plan. Remember, during the construction of your dream home, how there were unforeseen delays in the construction process as well as change-orders along the way? As you implement your strategic plan, we know for sure something in the internal environment or the external environment will change along the way, and you'll have to adjust your plan accordingly to stay on track to your target.

6. Evaluating Results (Implementation–Feedback–Adjust Loop)

This step should be called the *Feedback Loop* and applies to nearly everything you do, not just a strategic plan. Have you ever gone to a gun range to shoot a rifle or handgun? When you do, you intend to hit the bullseye of your target. You carefully line-up the sights, align the sights on the bullseye, and slowly squeeze the trigger until you send a round downrange toward the target. You started with the best of intentions and performed all of the mechanics precisely as your instructor told you to do. Now that you've pulled the trigger (implementation), you turn and walk away without getting any feedback on the results of your efforts. You merely assume you hit the bullseye because that was your intention, and you performed all the mechanics as instructed. Without feedback, you'd probably think you're the best marksman in the world. The same is true in the business world. You implemented your strategic plan with the best of intentions and performed all of the mechanics correctly. Or perhaps you issued a new policy/directive with the intent of creating some specific change in the workplace. But without a feedback loop, you will never know if your intention was accomplished at the line level, where the rubber meets the road.

Now, revisiting the gun range example, before you can get out the door, the rangemaster gives you feedback on the one shot you fired. The rangemaster says, "Hey buddy, you missed the bullseye. Instead, you hit the seven-ring, you're lucky your shot even hit the paper." Now, with this new information you just gained from the feedback loop, you return to the firing line, make some adjustments to the mechanics of your efforts based on the new data you just learned, and try again. You keep repeating this cycle until you successfully hit the bullseye.

Your work environment should use the same Implementation—Feedback—Adjust loop. You perform your executive-level function (whether that's implementing a strategic plan or issuing new policies) with the best of intentions. You implement the plan or issue the new policy, and then get feedback to make sure the real-life outcomes are consistent with your original intentions. If the outcomes are not consistent, you make adjustments, and try again. You keep repeating this cycle until the outcomes match your original intentions. When they match, that's called success. Comparing outcomes with your original intentions takes us to a critically important concept for executive-level leaders: Focusing on outcomes.

CHAPTER 26
Focusing on Outcomes

If you want quality work from a carpenter, it makes no sense to demand that he or she drill a certain number of holes or hammer a quota of nails. The essence of craftsmanship involves mastery of all the tools and the ability to select among them based on a clear understanding of the specific task at hand. Functional quotas make little sense in this context. This is where the strong leader, as mentioned earlier, focuses on outcomes. Tell your people what you want them to accomplish and get out of their way. To do anything else is considered micromanagement. Remember earlier when that was one of the top two complaints from employees? Focusing on outcomes is the way to eliminate micromanagement from your organization. Let me give you an example of how a great leader can sometimes get caught up in micromanagement.

There is a police chief I know and highly respect. I think this chief is the best law enforcement leader I have ever met. For the sake of the industry, I wish there was a way to clone him and distribute him throughout the industry—he's that good, and leaders like him are that rare.

However, one day, this chief issued a new directive. The new directive stated, from this point forward, all patrol officers will make at least fifteen traffic stops per month. For just a moment, let's discuss the dangers in a directive like that.

One danger in setting enforcement goals like this is it may bias the judgment of police officers in potentially dangerous ways and may contribute to aggressive or oppressive police conduct. It may incline officers to stretch the limits of legality and fairness for the sake of another arrest or ticket. Officers under stress to meet this new criterion may start making traffic stops for minor equipment violations they would otherwise not conduct. This will likely irritate citizens who are being stopped for seemingly petty violations—which will only serve to alienate the community. It's liable to produce quantity without regard to quality, relevance, or side effects. It undermines the importance of discretion and judgment exercised at the front line. It's no different from telling the carpenter how many nails to hammer or how many holes to drill.

I can tell you from working in the industry for so long; there will be officers who will respond, "Only 15 traffic stops per month? I do more than that in one week." Other officers who are not motivated by traffic stops will complain and may engage in malicious compliance and complete all 15 traffic stops in one day. It's also very likely all 15 stops will be for petty violations.

Considering all these potential side effects, is this outcome consistent with the chief's original intentions? What outcome did the chief really want? What the chief really wanted was more police visibility in an area where the trendline data indicated crime rates were increasing. You don't need to have any experience in the law enforcement industry to answer my next question. Are traffic stops the only way to increase police visibility in a particular area? Obviously, the answer is no. As I said, there will be officers who are already making that many good-quality traffic stops for inherently dangerous violations, and more. But other officers will be more inclined to get out of their cars and meet business owners and engage citizens on the sidewalk in conversation. Officers can be very creative if you ask them to suggest effective techniques to increase visibility in an area. Let them work their magic. As General George Patton said, tell them what you want them to accomplish (the outcome) and get out of their way, their ingenuity will amaze you. What the chief should have done would have been to convey the outcome he wanted and ask the technicians for ideas on the best ways to accomplish that outcome, and ideas on how to measure effectiveness. Much like CEO Kelleher did at Southwest Airlines.

There are two lessons in this story. First, even the best of leaders can get caught up in the details rather than focusing on outcomes. That's why a leader needs to have trusted advisors who the leader listens to when they say, "Hey boss, you need to focus on outcomes." And the second lesson is when you are a leader, you need to be focusing on the outcomes you want and avoid jumping back into the technician role. Avoid telling your technicians how many nails to hammer or how many holes to drill. If you study the great leaders in history, that's what they did—they focused on outcomes.

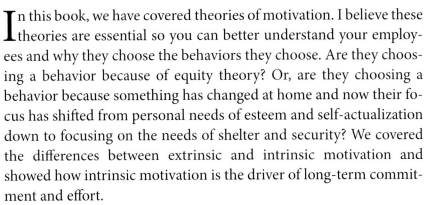

CHAPTER 27
Last Call

In this book, we have covered theories of motivation. I believe these theories are essential so you can better understand your employees and why they choose the behaviors they choose. Are they choosing a behavior because of equity theory? Or, are they choosing a behavior because something has changed at home and now their focus has shifted from personal needs of esteem and self-actualization down to focusing on the needs of shelter and security? We covered the differences between extrinsic and intrinsic motivation and showed how intrinsic motivation is the driver of long-term commitment and effort.

We also covered how we often confuse system problems with people problems and default to blaming the person when it's probably a systems problem. We covered how to recognize the red flags indicating a system may be broken or has substantial room for improvement, and we emphasized the importance of recognizing the trend line and not waiting for total system failure before taking corrective action.

In this book, we introduced the idea of executive-level leadership (aka organizational leadership) and how leadership at that level differs from interpersonal leadership. We covered many examples of how this higher-level leadership is extremely conceptual in nature, particularly in the need to have a vision for the future and how to articulate the image that exists in your mind's eye into words that formulate a vision statement.

This book introduced a high-level overview of how to create a strategic plan to make your vision a reality. The strategic plan also provides direction and accountability for your staff, which is a response to a significant complaint of employees—lack of direction.

Now let's reflect back to the original question at the beginning of this book: *Do employees have to bring motivation to the workplace, or does the workplace motivate the employee?* Here's my perspective on the answer. The workplace has a significant role in creating an environment that motivates the employee. The workplace does that by providing direction, by empowering employees, by embracing the importance of the employee's contribution toward mission accomplishment, and ultimately by providing a clear vision of where the organization aspires to go and what it aspires to accomplish in the future. The part the employee brings is a heartfelt connection with the vision and mission of the organization. Not everyone wants to be a police officer. Not everyone wants to be a doctor or nurse. Not everyone wants to be an architect. Every person is different, and everyone is inspired by different things. Some people are incredibly inspired by the vision of bringing clean drinking water to every person on the planet. The part the employee brings to the table is a heartfelt connection with your vision and mission. When your vision and mission statements are clear and compelling, and they connect with someone's heart, that is when people become committed to something bigger than themselves. The organization created that bigger thing. In my opinion, both the employee and the organization have their respective roles in creating motivation in the workplace.

Perhaps you disagree with me. That's fine. If you apply analytical thinking and can articulate a different perspective, then I have achieved my goal. In my role as an instructor in organizational leadership, there are two statements about education I subscribe to:

"Education is not the filling of a pail, but the lighting of a fire."
—W.B. Yeats

"Instruction should not be about dribbling drops of knowledge that students collect as they move from course to course. It should be more like gathering kindling, letting students play with matches, encouraging them to take risks, and hoping some of the materials burst into flames and become lifelong interests."

–Unknown

I hope the information in this book is merely the kindling in your journey as a life-long student of leadership. And whether you agree with my perspective or not, I hope you take this kindling and build a fire of your own.

In the introduction of this book, I said I live in a glass house. I confessed I was a poor leader, too. I also said when I realized I was a poor leader, I put my ego aside and worked hard to learn how to be a good leader. I went back to college and got a bachelor's degree and a master's degree in Management and Leadership. There was one person who played a crucial role in getting me back into school. His name is Dr. Dale Henry.

Dr. Henry is from Tennessee, and he was presenting a one-day seminar on leadership at the Washington State Criminal Justice Training Center in Burien, Washington. The date was January 27, 2012. The name of the seminar was Leadership Under Fire. As I mentioned early in this book, I did my best to attend anything with the word "leadership" in its title. Dr. Henry is a fabulous storyteller and kept the audience captivated for the entire day. But he said two things that day that changed the course of my life.

He said, "If you don't have your degree, you may be closer to getting it than you think." That sentence caught my attention because I had some college credits, but I didn't have a degree. He then said, "And if you don't get your degree, you're leaving money and opportunity on the table." At that moment, my ears must have tripled in size, like giant clown ears, because I wanted to hear more. Tell me, Dr. Henry, what do you mean by "leaving money and opportunity on the table?"

Within ten weeks, I was enrolled in an accelerated online program through Bluefield College, a brick and mortar college in Bluefield, Virginia. The program was called their Inspire program. It was an accelerated program where you completed your junior and senior years in one year. I was able to enroll with no money out-of-pocket. I'll explain how I did that a little later in this story.

I knew this window of academic opportunity was going to be short-lived, and I wanted to get everything out of the experience I could. So, I dove in head-first and committed every spare minute outside of my day job to this academic experience. I performed so well, every semester I was on the President's list. Not the Dean's list, but the highly esteemed President's list. Twelve months later, I had my bachelor's degree in Management and Leadership.

As soon as I graduated with my bachelor's degree, I enrolled in an online master's program through Western Governor's University–Washington. I repeated my commitment of diving in head-first with every spare minute I could muster. Western Governor's University is a work-at-your-own-speed college. Fifteen months later, I had my master's degree in Management and Leadership.

When I first enrolled at Bluefield College, they gave me a lot of credit for the training classes I had as a police officer. I already had some college credits, which were applied to my degree, but I also needed some additional English credits. A counselor suggested I go to the University of Washington to take a test to challenge the English class—which I did. I passed the challenge test, which allowed me to stay on my schedule for graduation and save money at the same time.

Here's the explanation you've been waiting for regarding the financial part of my academic experience. At the time, my employer reimbursed 80% of tuition costs for a bachelor's degree. At Bluefield College, the e-textbooks were included in the tuition, so there was no additional cost for textbooks. The college admissions office helped get me set up with student loans for my first semester. As a result, I paid zero to get enrolled in college. At the end of the semester, I submitted my grades to my HR department and in return, I received a check for 80% of my tuition costs. I promptly used that check to pay my student loan. I then paid the remaining 20% out of my pocket, plus a minimal finance charge on the loan for the semester. Then I repeated the cycle for the next semester.

When I enrolled for my master's degree, the situation was much different, but not in the way I expected. My employer only reimbursed 40% of tuition costs for a master's degree. I repeated the cycle by getting a student loan for the first semester's tuition. At the end of the first semester, I submitted my grades to HR, expecting a check for 40% of the tuition costs, but instead I received a check for 100% of my tuition. I was confused; this had to be some sort of mistake. I took the check to HR and they explained the reimbursement rate is based on the state tuition rate of the University of Washington, and they reimburse 40% of that rate. However, the tuition rate at Western Governor's University was only one-third of the rate U of W charges, so 100% of my tuition was below the 40% threshold. Every semester I got a check for 100% of my tuition, which I immediately used to repay my student loan, and then only paid a nominal finance charge out of my own pocket. My master's degree was virtually free.

Here's my takeaway on those comments made by Dr. Henry back on that fateful day of January 27, 2012, which changed the course of my life. Through online classes, higher-level education is more accessible than it's ever been before. The time you can save in commuting back and forth to a brick-and-mortar classroom can be time well spent toward studying instead of sitting in traffic. If your employer offers a tuition reimbursement program, that is money your employer is willing to give to you—*if* you go to school. If you don't go to school, you are just leaving that money on the table—or in your employer's pocket. Also, in my case, if you possess a bachelor's degree, my employer increased my salary by 2% and by 4% for a master's degree. Again, that is money the employer is willing to put in your pocket *if* you get a degree. If you don't, you just leave that money in the employer's pocket.

Additionally, if nothing else, getting your degree in any field enhances your critical thinking skills, making you more valuable in any work environment. For me, entering the academic experience later in life was far more valuable because I had years of real-life work experience to compare to what I was learning in the classroom. I could picture real-life experiences and relate those experiences to the curriculum. As a result, everything had far more meaning and value than it would have had if I had taken the same classes when I was fresh out of high school.

I tell this story in every class I teach because I want to encourage leaders of tomorrow to obtain higher-level education if they don't already have it. As Dr. Henry said, "if you don't have your degree, you may be closer to getting it than you think." And, "if you don't get your degree, you're leaving money and opportunity on the table." I explain to my students that if they have college-age children of their own who have tuition reimbursement available to them through the child's employer, and they aren't taking advantage of it, as a parent they'll be kicking their children in the hind-end (figuratively) to get themselves into school. This is my "kick in your hind-end" for you to do the same—regardless of your age. I was in my 50s when I went back to school. By the way, I sent Dr. Henry a thank you email for his life-changing words that day back in 2012. I wanted him to know those words made a difference in at least one person's life, and I'm confident they made a difference in many other lives as well. The bottom line is this: As a leader, you should be a life-long learner. If you don't have your degree yet, start researching your options; you may be closer than you think.

If you take nothing else away from this book, I hope at a minimum you take away these four points:

1. As upper-level management, your role in organizational leadership is much different than it was at lower levels in the organization where interpersonal leadership was the norm. Remember, interpersonal leadership is still significant at the executive level, but you also need to add in the conceptual part of *organizational leadership*. That's where the direction for the organization and guidance for your staff originates.

2. Focus on outcomes. You are no longer the technician; you are the leader who focuses on outcomes. Don't tell your people how many nails to hammer, or how many holes to drill. Tell your people what you want them to accomplish and get out of their way because their ingenuity will amaze you.

3. Create a compelling vision statement and mission statement. People who believe in what you believe about the future of your organization will be knocking down your door to work for you. Make sure everyone in the organization understands the value of their contribution to the organization and to the vision, just like the janitor at NASA. If the work they do doesn't provide some valuable contribution to the organization and the vision, that position would not be on the payroll—it's on the payroll because it provides value. Help them connect their work to the bigger picture; that connection creates strong intrinsic motivation and commitment.

4. The first responsibility of a leader is to define what can be. The last responsibility is to say, "Thank you." Remember to thank your followers for the contributions they make. Praise them for their hard work and commitment. Your praise is probably the most powerful, simplest, least costly, and yet most underused motivational technique there is. Your praise fulfills your employee's need for esteem, self-actualization, growth, and achievement. Always remember to say, "Thank you."

Now I have one final request of you. Go forth and…

Lead, Teach, and Inspire.

INDEX

Symbols

A

B

C

D

E

F

G

H

I